OXFORD

geog.2

geography for key sta

D1341028

< rosemarie gallagher > < richard parish >

OXFORD
UNIVERSITY PRESS

Great Clarendon Street, Oxford OX2 6DP

Oxford University Press is a department of the University of Oxford.
It furthers the University's objective of excellence in research,
scholarship, and education by publishing worldwide in

Oxford New York

Auckland Bangkok Buenos Aires Cape Town Chennai
Dar es Salaam Delhi Hong Kong Istanbul Karachi Kolkata
Kuala Lumpur Madrid Melbourne Mexico City Mumbai
Nairobi São Paulo Shanghai Taipei Tokyo Toronto

Oxford is a registered trade mark of Oxford University Press
in the UK and in certain other countries

British Library Cataloguing in Publication Data

Data available

ISBN 0 19 913414 6

10 9 8

Printed in Italy by Rotolito Lombarda.

Acknowledgements

The Publisher would like to thank the following for permission to reproduce
photographs:

Chapter 1 Aerofilms: pp. 9, 11 (bottom), 15; Corbis UK Ltd – Cordaily Picture
Library: p. 5 (bottom right): Owen Franken: p. 7 (both); Nik Wheeler: p. 8; Corel
Professional Photos: p. 5 (top left); Environmental Images/Martin Bond: p. 11
(top); Getty One Stone: p. 4 (bottom left); Robert Harding Picture Library –
David Hughes: p. 4 (bottom right); Roy Rainford: p. 4 (top left); High-Point
Rendel: p. 16 (top); Tony Lees: p. 13 (middle & bottom), 21; National Trust –
Geoff Morgan: p. 5 (top right); Neil Rainey: p. 13 (top): Press Association – John
Giles: pp. 16 (bottom), 18; Chris Ison: p. 20; Sealand Aerial Photography: p. 19.
Chapter 2 Century Litho Ltd:p. 28 (bottom); Corbis UK Ltd – Paul Almassy:
p. 40 (top); Richard Bickel: p. 40 (bottom); Tony Arruza: p. 23 (right; Cordaily
Picture Library: p. 35; Fotografia: p. 36 (left); Richard Hamilton Smith: p. 41
(middle riight); Wild Country: p. 24 (top); Corel Professional Photos: pp. 23
(left), 26 (main, bottom left, right and middle), 36 (right), 41 (left, left middle
& right); Eurosat: pp. 32 (bottom), 33; Martin Sookias: p. 26 (top); Getty One
Stone: p. 34 (top); The Met Office: p. 24 (bottom left); Mirror Syndication:
p. 28 (top); John Walmsley: p. 24 (bottom right). **Chapter 3** Corbis UK Ltd –
O Alamany & E Vicens: p. 55 (top left); Michael Busselle: p. 42; FLPA/Pam
Gardner: p. 51 (left); Wolfgang Kaehler: p. 55 (middle right); Buddy Mays:
pp. 51 (right), 54; Keren Su: p. 47 (bottom); Corel Professional Photos: p. 48
(bottom left); The Image Bank: p. 53 (middle); R O Barnes, Kenya Archives:
p. 58 (left); Michael Mortimore: p. 58 (right); Oxford Scientific Films – Kathie
Atkinson: pp. 45, 48 (top right); Terry Heathcote: p. 48 (bottom right); Andrew
Park: p. 48 (top left); Sealand Aerial Photography: p. 47 (top); Still Pictures –
Mark Edwards: p. 57 (right); David Hoffman: p. 53 (bottom); Mathieu
Laboureur: p. 55 (top right); Muriel Nicolotti: p. 55 (bottom right); Jorgen Scatte:
p. 57 (left); USGS/Earthshots: p. 53 (top).

Chapter 4 Corbis UK Ltd – Yann Arthus-Bertrand: p. 62 (middle and right); Jack
Fields: p. 65; Wolfgang Kaehler: p. 66; Corel Professional Photos: p. 62 (left);
Martin Sookias: p. 64. **Chapter 5** Center for Research and Studies on Kuwait:
p. 74 (top left & right); Corbis UK Ltd – Chromo Sohm Inc.: p. 83; Hulton: p. 77
(bottom); Roger Ressmeyer: p. 82 (top right); Corel Professional Photos: p. 72
(top); GeoAtlas: p. 78; Greenpeace/Beltra: p. 79; Illustrated London News: p. 70;
NREL: pp. 82 (top middle, middle left & right, bottom left, middle & right), 84
(both), 85 (all); Press Association/EPA: pp. 74 (bottom), 77 (top); Still
Pictures/Mark Edwards: p. 72 (bottom); Martin Sookias: p. 82 (top left).
Chapter 6 Barnaby's Picture Library: pp. 90 (top right), 95 (middle); Corbis UK
Ltd – Art on File: p. 90 (bottom right); Rik Ergenbright: p. 96 (bottom middle;
Eye Ubiquitous/Patrick Field: p. 96 (top right); Gallo Images/Paul Velasco: p. 94
(top left); Francis de Mulder: p. 96 (top left); Purcell Team: p. 90 (bottom left);
Bill Varie: p. 95 (bottom); Michael Yamashita: pp. 90 (top right), 96 (bottom
left); Inge Yspeert: p. 90 (middle left); CR World: pp. 87, 93 (bottom); Format
Photographers – Jackie Chapman: p. 86 (top); Joanne O'Brian: p. 86 (bottom);
London Aerial Photo Library: pp. 88, 90 (top middle & middle right); OUP:
p. 94 (bottom); Photofusion/Ute Klaphake: p. 96 (bottom right); Popperfoto:
p. 97; Press Association/EPA: p. 96 (top middle); Martin Sookias: pp. 90
(centre), 93 (top), 94 (top right), 95 (top), 97 (bottom); Still Pictures/Mark
Edwards: p. 90 (bottom middle). **Chapter 7** Corbis UK Ltd – Yann Artus-
Bertrand: pp. 100 (top left), 102 (bottom left), 113; Jonathan Blair: p. 98 (top
middle); Tom Brakefield: p. 98 (top left); Jan Butchovsky-Houser: p. 100 (middle
right); Ecoscene/Joel Creed: p. 100 (top right); Robert Holmes: p. 117; Dave
Houser: pp. 99 (top), 108 (right; Daniel Laire: p. 104; Richard List: p. 108 (left);
Massimo Listi: p. 98 bottom middle right); Stephanie Maze: pp. 105, 119 (left),
119 (bottom); Purcell Team: p. 110 (bottom); Julia Waterlow: p. 119 (right);
Corel Professional Photos: pp. 98 (top & bottom right), 99 (bottom left), 100
(bottom right), 102 (top left), 107 (bottom), 111, 118 (top); Getty One Stone:
p. 98 (top middle right); Robert Harding Picture Library: p. 98 (middle & bottom
left), 107 (top); The Image Bank: pp. 110 (top), 115 (left); South American
Pictures – Jason Howe: p. 99 (bottom right); Tony Morrison: pp. 102 (middle &
right bottom), 106, 115 (right), 118 (bottom).

The Ordnance Survey map extract on p. 13 is reproduced with the permission
of the Controller of Her Majesty's Stationery Office © Crown Copyright

Illustrations are by James Alexander, Alan Baker; Jeff Bowles, Stefan Chabluk,
William Donohoe, Michael Eaton, Antonia Enthoven, Hardlines, John Hallett,
Roger Kent, Erin Kirke, David Mostyn, Richard Morris, Colin Salmon and Martin
Sanders.

With special thanks to Charles Stanley & Company Ltd, Oxford.

The publisher and authors would like to thank all the individuals and
organizations who have helped during research for this book. In particular, and
following the topic order: Margaret Freer of the Sustainable Development Unit,
East Riding of Yorkshire Council; Chris Matthews, formerly Principal Officer
(Strategy), East Riding of Yorkshire Council and now with Scarborough Borough
Council; Steve Fort and Corinne Locker of High-Point Rendel; Medea Gravelle,
Coastal Strategy Officer for Dorset Coastal Forum; George Anderson and Sean
Clarke of the Met.Office; Eileen Anne Millar, Professor of Italian, University of
Glasgow; James Lovelock; Michael Mortimore; Alex 'Walter' Middleton; the
Energy Policy and Analysis Unit at the DTI; Jack Stone of the National
Renewable Energy Laboratory, USA; Akanksha Chaurey of the Tata Energy
Research Institute, New Delhi; Omar Farooque; Dr Nick Fyfe of the Department
of Geography, University of Dundee; Chris Morris, GIS Analyst at Brent Council;
Phil Spivey and Martin Garrad of the Community Safety Department, Sussex
Police; Jane Oakland of Wembley Police; Nelson Lafraia and Maurizina Foulkes
of the Brazilian Embassy, London; Deísa Holden; Silvia and Penny Aldersley.

We would like to thank our excellent reviewers who have provided thoughtful
and constructive criticism at various stages: Phyl Gallagher, Anna King, Roger
Fetherston, and Philip Amor.

We would particularly like to thank Janet Williamson for her contribution to this
book and her overall contribution to the geog.123 course.

Every effort has been made to contact copyright holders of material reproduced
in this book. Any omissions will be rectified in subsequent printings if notice is
given to the publisher.

Layout by Zed, Oxford.

Contents

Off to the coast

Wherever you live in the UK, you are never more than a few hours from the **coast**. Look at these photos.

▲ *South Stack, Anglesey.*

ATLANTIC OCEAN

SCOTLAND

North Sea

NORTHERN IRELAND

REPUBLIC OF IRELAND

Irish Sea

WALES

ENGLAND

English Channel

▲ *Kynance Cove, Cornwall.*

▲ *White Nothe, Dorset.*

▲ *Stonehaven, Aberdeenshire.*

▲ *Morston Marshes, Norfolk.*

Did you know?
◆ The UK's coastline is 12 430 km long.
◆ The straight line distance from London to New York is 5530 km!

All change!

The places in these photos all look different. But they have one thing in common. They are all changing slowly, day by day, because of the sea. You will find out how in later units.

▲ *Brighton beach, Sussex.*

Your turn

1 Look at the photos on page 4.
   a Which of these places do you like best? Draw a labelled sketch of it.
   b Now write a postcard message to send from that place to your friend in New York.

2 Which of the photos A–F show sand? Where do you think this sand came from?

3 Which place in the photos do you think gets the strongest waves? Say what clues you used.

4 See if you can explain why:
   a there is a lighthouse at the place shown in A.
   b Brighton, in F, is a seaside resort.
   c the place shown in A is not a seaside resort.
   d the place shown in A is famous for the colonies of sea birds that nest there.
   e Stonehaven, in D, has built those concrete piers.

5 Around the coast you'll find different types of rock. Look at photos B, C and E. See if you can match them to these rock types:
   chalk   granite   clay
   Give reasons for your choice.

6 People like to go to the coast for holidays. Write a list of outdoor sports and other activities you can do at the coast. The photos will help a little.

7 Brighton is a seaside resort. See if you can name:
   a three other UK seaside resorts b three UK ports
   The map on page 121 may help.

8 Now write a list of jobs that depend on the sea and the seaside. (At least six.)

9 Here in the UK, we are living on an island. Give:
   a three advantages b three disadvantages
   of living on an island.

Waves and tides

Waves and tides make the coast exciting – and dangerous!

What causes waves?

Waves are caused by the **wind** dragging on the surface of the water.
The length of water the wind blows over is called its **fetch**.

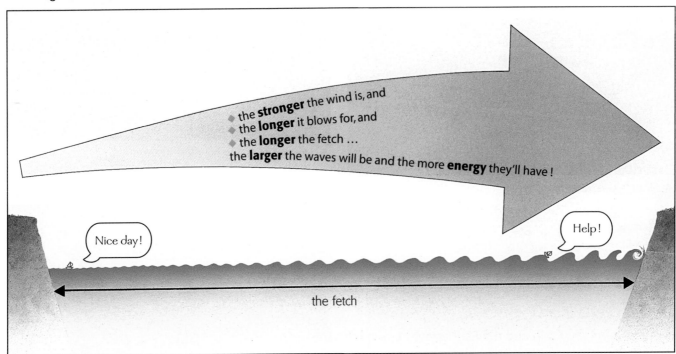

- the **stronger** the wind is, and
- the **longer** it blows for, and
- the **longer** the fetch ...

the **larger** the waves will be and the more **energy** they'll have!

Nice day!

Help!

the fetch

When waves reach the coast

Swash this then?

Backwash!

Out at sea, the waves roll like this. In a gale they can be over 30 metres high!

They break in shallow water, like this. The water that rushes up the sand is called the **swash**.

The water rolling back into the sea – like this – is called the **backwash**.

If the backwash has more energy than the swash the waves eat at the land, dragging pebbles and sand away. (This happens with high steep waves.)
But if the swash has more energy than the backwash, material is carried on to the land and left there. (This happens with low flat waves.)

Tides

Even when the sea is calm and flat, the water level is always changing. That's mainly because of the moon. As it travels around the Earth it attracts the sea and pulls it upwards. (The sun helps too, but it is much further from the Earth so its pull is not so strong.)

The rise and fall of the sea gives us the **tides**. Look at these photos:

Tuesday 9.00 am. The tide is **in** at this coastal town. In fact the sea has reached its highest level for today. This is called **high tide**.

Same day, 3.20 pm. Now the tide is **out**, leaving the boats resting on the mud. The sea has fallen to its lowest level for the day. This is called **low tide**.

High tides occur about every twelve and a half hours, with low tides in between. But the rise and fall is a little different each time. That's because the combined pull of the sun and moon keeps changing, as the moon moves around the Earth and the Earth moves around the sun.

Your turn

1 The arrows are winds blowing onto island X.

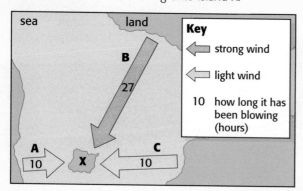

Which winds will produce:
a the largest waves   b the smallest waves
  at the coast of X? Explain your answers.

2 Write out each word from list A with its correct meaning from list B.

A	B
fetch	runs down the sand after a wave breaks
swash	the length of water the wind blows over
backwash	the result of the rise and fall in sea level
tides	rushes up the sand when a wave breaks

3 A post was placed in the sea near the town above, to show the heights of the tides. This drawing shows readings for 23 July.
  a Why did the water level change?
  b Copy and complete this table to show how the water level changed:

metres
6 —
5 —
← 8.15 pm
4 — ← 7.35 am
3 —
2 — ← 1.05 am
1 — ← 1.25 pm
0 —

From	the tide
1.05 am to 7.35 am	rose by 2.0 metres
7.35 am to 1.25 pm	
1.25 pm to 8.15 pm	

  c Why was the second rise greater?

4 Look at photo C on page 4. Was it taken at high tide? How can you tell?

5 Now look at photo A on page 4. You are on holiday on Anglesey. Two days ago you were scrambling around on the rocks – and got trapped at X by high tide! Write a really exciting entry for your diary saying how you felt and how you were saved.

1.3 The waves at work

Waves have energy. That means they can work. They work non-stop, night and day, shaping the coastline.

What do the waves do?

Waves do the same kind of work as rivers do.

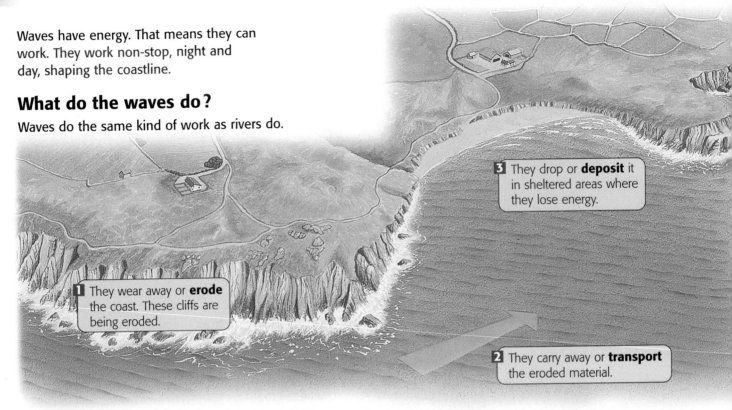

3 They drop or **deposit** it in sheltered areas where they lose energy.

1 They wear away or **erode** the coast. These cliffs are being eroded.

2 They carry away or **transport** the eroded material.

Now we will look at each of these in more detail.

Erosion

This is how waves wear away the coast:

They hammer against the rock. The pressure can be as much as 30 tonnes a square metre. Over time, this breaks the rock up.

They force water into cracks in the rock, under pressure. This helps to break the rock up. It is called **hydraulic action**.

The water dissolves soluble material from the rock. This is called **solution**.

The waves fling sand, pebbles and large stones against the rock. These wear it away like sandpaper. This is called **abrasion**.

Chunks of rock get knocked together and worn into smaller and smaller bits. This is called **attrition**. They end up as **shingle** (pebbles) and **sand**.

The more energy the waves have, and the softer the rock, the faster erosion will be.

Transport

The waves carry the eroded material away. Some is carried right out to sea. But a lot is carried *along* the coastline. Like this …

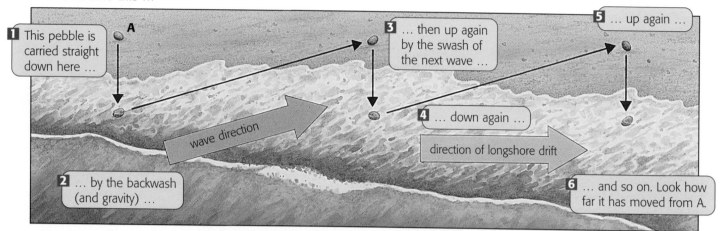

1 This pebble is carried straight down here …

2 … by the backwash (and gravity) …

3 … then up again by the swash of the next wave …

4 … down again …

5 … up again …

6 … and so on. Look how far it has moved from A.

wave direction

direction of longshore drift

In this way, hundreds of thousands of tonnes of pebbles and sand get moved along our coastline every year. This movement is called **longshore drift**.

Many seaside towns build **groynes** to stop their beaches being carried away by longshore drift. Look at this photo.

Deposition

Waves continually carry material on and off the land. If they carry more *on* than *off* – a beach forms! Some beaches are made of sand. Some are made of **shingle** or small pebbles.

Beaches grow in sheltered areas. Low flat waves carry material up the beach and leave it there.

a groyne

N

▲ *Without the groynes – hardly any beach!*

Your turn

1 Waves do three jobs that shape the coastline. Name them.

2 List three ways in which waves erode rock.

3 These pebbles are made of the same rock.
   a Which has been in the water longer? Explain.
   b Name the process that made Y so smooth.

4 Look at the groynes in the photo above.
   a Why were they built?
   b Are they working? How can you tell?
   c From which direction do the waves usually arrive at this beach?
      i from the south west
      ii from the south east
   Give a reason for your choice.

5

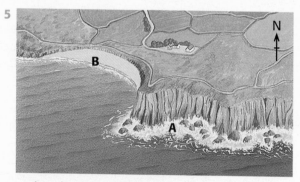

B

A

N

Look at the drawing above.

a The *prevailing wind* is blowing. What does that mean? From which direction does it blow?

b From which direction do the waves usually arrive?

c There is no beach at A. Suggest a reason.

d There is a good beach at B. Give a reason.

e Where might the sand at B have come from?

Landforms created by the waves

Day and night, the waves are hard at work. They erode material from some parts of the coast, and deposit it in other parts. That's how they create different landforms.

This coast is made of different rocks, some hard, some soft. Once upon a time it was straight. Just look at it now:

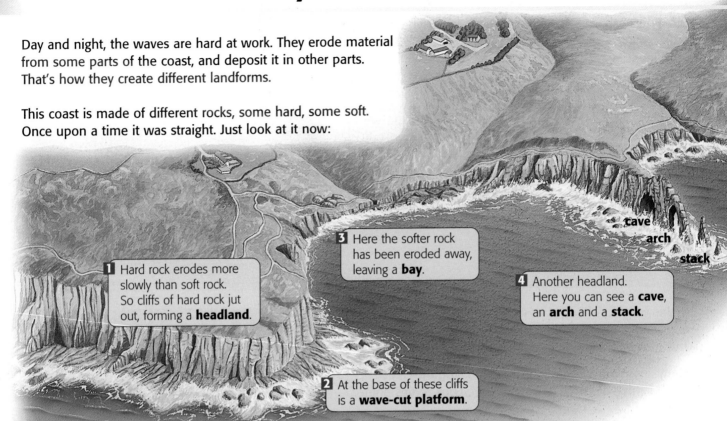

1 Hard rock erodes more slowly than soft rock. So cliffs of hard rock jut out, forming a **headland**.

2 At the base of these cliffs is a **wave-cut platform**.

3 Here the softer rock has been eroded away, leaving a **bay**.

4 Another headland. Here you can see a **cave**, an **arch** and a **stack**.

cave
arch
stack

How a wave-cut platform forms

  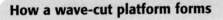

1 The waves carve **wave-cut notches** into cliffs at a headland. These get deeper and deeper …

2 … until, one day, the rock above them collapses. The sea carries the debris away.

3 The process continues non-stop. Slowly the cliffs retreat, leaving a **wave-cut platform** behind.

How caves, arches and stacks form

1 The sea attacks cracks in the cliff at a headland. The cracks grow larger – and form a **cave**.

2 The cave gets eroded all the way through. It turns into an **arch**. Then one day …

3 … the arch collapses, leaving a **stack**. In time, the waves erode the stack to a **stump**.

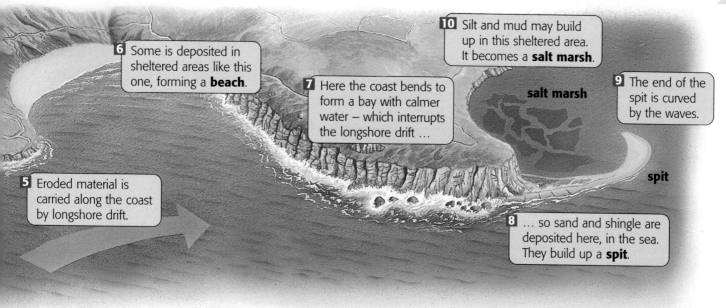

6 Some is deposited in sheltered areas like this one, forming a **beach**.

7 Here the coast bends to form a bay with calmer water – which interrupts the longshore drift …

10 Silt and mud may build up in this sheltered area. It becomes a **salt marsh**.

salt marsh

9 The end of the spit is curved by the waves.

5 Eroded material is carried along the coast by longshore drift.

spit

8 … so sand and shingle are deposited here, in the sea. They build up a **spit**.

Your turn

1

Landform	Created by ...	
	erosion	deposition
headland	✓	

Make a table like the one started here. Write in the names of all the landforms you met in this unit. Then put a ✓ to show how each was formed.

2 Make a larger sketch of the landforms in photo A.
  a On your sketch, label:
    a wave-cut notch   an arch   a stump
  b Explain how the arch was formed.
  c Draw a dotted line to show where there was once another arch.
  d What will happen to the stump over time?

3 Photo B shows the spit at Dawlish Warren in Devon.
  a Make a sketch of the spit.
  b From which direction does the prevailing wind blow? Mark this on your sketch.
  c Mark an X at three points where the wind (and waves) changed direction for a period.

4

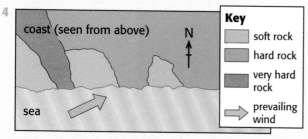

	Key	
coast (seen from above) N↑		soft rock
		hard rock
		very hard rock
sea →		prevailing wind

This is part of the coast, *before* erosion. Make a larger drawing to show how it may look 10 000 years from now. Label any landforms you show.

A

B

Along the Dorset coast

The OS map opposite shows part of the south coast of England, in Dorset. Study the map and the photos. Then try these questions. The key on page 120 will help.

Your turn

1 Photos A–C were taken at sites on the map.
   a Write two sentences for each photo, to describe what it shows.
   b Now match each photo to one of these grid references: 028862   054825   042787
   008788   031835   036788
   You'll find grid numbers marked on the map – but not along the edges!

2 Find three clues on the map, to show that:
   a this is a historic area
   b Swanage is now a seaside resort.
   For each clue, give a six-figure grid reference.

3 Longshore drift is a problem at Swanage.
   How can you tell this from the map?

4 The map below shows the **geology** of the area – what kind of rocks it is made of.
   a What kind of rock is Old Harry (055825) made of?
   b What kind of rock is Furzey Island made of?
   c Give a six-figure grid reference for a farm where the soil is clay.
   d Which two types of rock seem hardest to erode? Explain your choice.
   e What clue is there that clay is easy to erode?

5 Pick out the rectangle on the OS map with corners at 020830, 020870, 050870 and 050830. Draw a sketch map of this area, showing the *main* features. Such as the dunes, the sea, woodland – but not the phone box.

6 These are old maps of the area you sketched in 5.

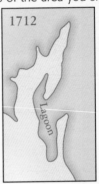

   a As you can see, the shape has changed a lot over the years. Suggest reasons. (Hint: any sign of spits?)
   b Now explain how Little Sea (on your sketch map) has been formed over the years since 1849.

7 You are staying with a group at the camp site at Ulwell. It's summer. The weather is fine. You have to plan a long walk for the group. These are the rules:

> ◆ If possible, use footpaths rather than roads.
> ◆ You may join the South West Coast Path.
> ◆ Include a visit to a nature reserve.
> ◆ Include a walk along the beach.
> ◆ Give the group a good view of arches and stacks.
> ◆ Let them look over a steep cliff.
> ◆ Return to the camp site by a different route.

   a Draw a sketch map for your planned route, showing:
   i the coastline
   ii your route
   iii the coastal landforms you'll see on the walk
   iv any ancient sites you will pass
   v any other points of interest
   b Mark any places where the walk may be extra difficult or dangerous. Add a note to say why.
   c Work out roughly how long each section of the walk will be. Mark it on your map.
   d And finally, make a list of what to take with you.

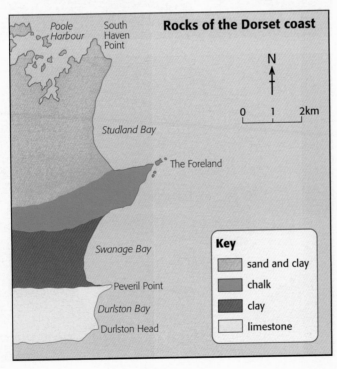

Rocks of the Dorset coast

Poole Harbour
South Haven Point
N
0 1 2km
Studland Bay
The Foreland
Swanage Bay
Peveril Point
Durlston Bay
Durlston Head

Key
sand and clay
chalk
clay
limestone

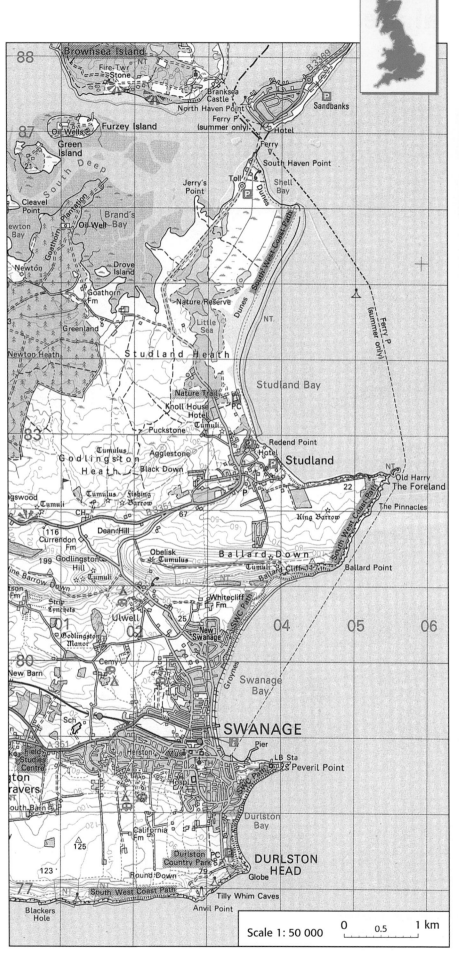

Scale 1: 50 000

0   0.5   1 km

Did you know?

◆ In 878, King Alfred defeated the Danes in a fierce sea battle off Swanage.

THE NATIONAL TRUST

STUDLAND HEATH

How we use coastal areas

Oh we do love to be beside the seaside!

But if we all did as we pleased along the coast, there would be chaos.
So the coast has to be **managed**. That means people have to agree on
a plan for the best way to use it, and then put the plan into action.

Who manages our coastal areas?

The coast, like the rest of the UK, is managed mostly by **local councils**.
These are made up of local people. (When you are 18 you can vote
for your local council.)

Suppose you want to build a new golf course or hotel along the coast.
This is what to do:

> **Did you know?**
> ◆ You can own land along the coast – but not under the sea.
> ◆ The sea bed and land below high tide belong to the Crown.

Send your plan to
the local council,
and ask for planning
permission.

The council may like
the plan. But it still has
to send out notices
asking if anyone objects.

A **public inquiry**
may be held, where
people come to state
their objections.

An inspector will
study the objections,
and decide if the
plan can go ahead.

Sometimes, for big projects, the government gets involved.
It can over-rule the council and turn down a plan, or agree to it.

Your turn

1.

Work	Leisure
farming	walking

Make a table like this to show how the coast is used. Write in all the activities shown in the drawing on page 14.

2. This grid shows some of the people in the drawing.

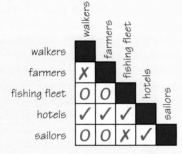

a. The ✗ shows that farmers and walkers may come into conflict with each other. Give a reason.

b. The ✓ shows that the hotels and fishing fleet may benefit each other. Explain why.

c. The O shows that sailors and walkers do not affect each other. Why?

3. a. Draw your own grid for the people in the drawing. (Your table for question 1 will help.)

b. Fill in a ✓, ✗ or O in each empty square.

c. For each conflict (✗), suggest a way to solve the problem.

4. Now turn to the OS map on page 13. What activities take place in this coastal area? Look for clues, and give four-figure grid references.

5. Dream Developments wants to build a leisure complex on the Dorset coast. See the photos of the site and the drawing of the complex, below.

a. Identify their chosen site on the map on page 13, and try to give a 6-figure grid reference for it.

b. What is the site used for at the moment?

6. You are the head of Dream Developments. Write a letter to the council to say how your plan will help the area. For example you could mention:
   ◆ how good the complex will look
   ◆ how you can provide work for local people.

7. List any bad points about the leisure complex. For example think about how it might affect:
   wildlife   the scenery   traffic in the area

8. *Do you* think the leisure complex should go ahead? Write a speech for the public enquiry, stating your opinion. Give your main reasons (no more than three).

the proposed site

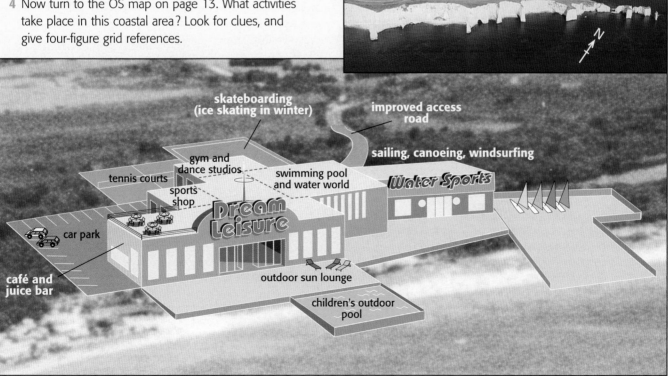

Cliff collapse !

All round the coast, cliffs are being eaten away by waves and weathering. Some get so weak they collapse. And that means trouble!

Landslip brings hotel to the brink

Last night a four-star hotel was falling inch by inch into the sea, after a cliff collapsed at Scarborough, North Yorkshire.

Twenty-four hours earlier, the 100-year-old Holbeck Hall had stood 50 metres from the cliff edge, amid rose gardens and perfect lawns. By dawn yesterday it was poised on the brink of the cliff. In the afternoon it began slowly toppling over.

Eighty guests in the £100-a-night hotel were roused from their beds shortly before breakfast yesterday and told to get ready to leave. But as they packed their cases the lawn dropped by 4 metres, and the manager ordered them out immediately.

By late afternoon a conservatory, sun lounge and new restaurant had gone. Later the lintel over the main door cracked and a large window above it shattered. Next a gable collapsed, sending bricks, metal, glass, chimney pots and other rubble onto the drive. The landslip took a huge bite over 100m wide and 250 m deep from the cliff, and poured a million tonnes of rock, clay and soil onto the beach below.

'In dry summers, cracks can develop in the clay cliffs', said an engineer from Scarborough Council. 'Then if you get a very wet winter, the water gets in through the cracks and lubricates the clay and that means trouble.'

From a newspaper article, 5 June 1993

▲ *Holbeck Hall before the fall. The hotel slid towards the sea.*

Why do cliffs collapse?

 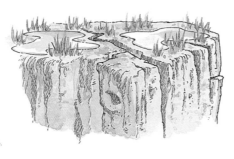 

Cliffs are eroded by the waves and weakened by weathering. For example rain soaks into the cracks in them and dissolves minerals …

… and in winter, ice makes cracks wider. So after heavy rain the cliffs may be full of water. The more water in them the weaker they are.

Clay cliffs are worst because rain makes clay very slippery. Huge blocks of clay just go sliding past each other down the slope.

Clay cliffs are a big problem – but *any* cliffs will collapse if they soak up enough water. One way to solve the problem is to bury pipes in them to carry the water away. But that costs a lot and the pipes won't last for ever.

Your turn

1 What is a landslip? If you don't know, guess.

2 What are the cliffs at Scarborough made of?

3 Explain what part these played in the loss of Holbeck Hall.
   a There had been several dry summers before 1993.
   b The spring of 1993 was very wet.

4 The landslip worried Scarborough Borough Council. Someone could have got killed! This diagram shows the work they got done in the following months to make the area safe. It cost around £1.5 million. Explain why each step A to H was taken.

5 The Holbeck Hall Hotel was built in 1880 as a house for a rich man called George Alderson Smith.
   a Why do people choose to live on top of cliffs?
   b It is 1879. You are Silas Kistle, a clever young engineer. You know a thing or two about cliffs! Write a letter to Mr Smith advising him not to build on this site, and saying why.

6 So what should we use cliff tops for? Should we ban people from building on them?
   Give your ideas in any form you wish.
   For example as a drawing, a radio interview, or a written report for Scarborough Borough Council.

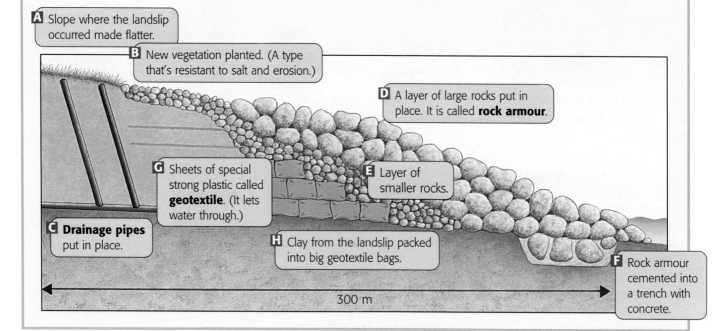

A Slope where the landslip occurred made flatter.

B New vegetation planted. (A type that's resistant to salt and erosion.)

D A layer of large rocks put in place. It is called **rock armour**.

G Sheets of special strong plastic called **geotextile**. (It lets water through.)

E Layer of smaller rocks.

C **Drainage pipes** put in place.

H Clay from the landslip packed into big geotextile bags.

F Rock armour cemented into a trench with concrete.

300 m

Waving goodbye to the Holderness coast?

Land disappears in great chunks when cliffs collapse. And more slowly, bit by bit, day by day. On parts of the Holderness coast in Yorkshire, the sea nibbles away around 8 mm of land (this much: ▬▬) each day. In the last 1000 years, 29 villages have gone.

Holderness

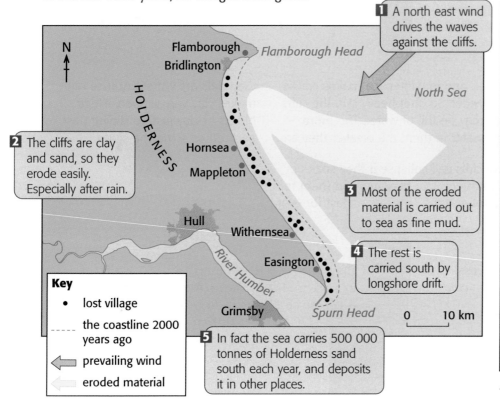

1 A north east wind drives the waves against the cliffs.

Flamborough Head

North Sea

Flamborough
Bridlington

HOLDERNESS

2 The cliffs are clay and sand, so they erode easily. Especially after rain.

Hornsea
Mappleton

3 Most of the eroded material is carried out to sea as fine mud.

Hull
Withernsea

4 The rest is carried south by longshore drift.

River Humber

Easington

Key
- • lost village
- ----- the coastline 2000 years ago
- ⇐ prevailing wind
- ⇐ eroded material

Grimsby   *Spurn Head*   0   10 km

5 In fact the sea carries 500 000 tonnes of Holderness sand south each year, and deposits it in other places.

N

▲ *Mappleton in 1990 – just hanging on.*

How can we stop the coast eroding?

We can build **sea walls** like this one, to stop the waves reaching the land …

… or a barrier of large rocks (**rock armour**) to soak up their energy. Less energy means less erosion.

We could even build the barrier out at sea, to make the waves break away from the shore.

Or build **groynes** to stop sand being carried away. The sand in turn protects the coast.

Or build up the beach by adding more sand or shingle. This is called **beach replenishment**.

Here today, gone tomorrow.

Or we could decide to do nothing at all, and let nature take its course …

So what did they do at Mappleton?

Look at Mappleton on page 18 – about to slide into the sea. But the people fought for a grant to protect their village. This photo shows the defences that were put in, in 1992. Not everyone was happy …

Your turn

1 Look at the photo of Mappleton on page 18.
   a What is happening to the land, and why?
   b Whose fault do you think it is?
   c Some sand from this land will end up on Spurn Head. Explain why. (Look at the map.)
   d Which type of landform is Spurn Head?

2 The photo above shows Mappleton in 1993, after action was taken to protect it from erosion.
   a What was done: at A? at B? at C?
   Explain how each will help to stop erosion.
   b Give a reason why a sea wall was *not* built at C.
   c Where will most sand build up in future?
   around A   around B   around C

3 There are reasons for and against protecting the coast from erosion. Give:
   a one *economic* reason *for* protecting it (Glossary?)
   b one *environmental* reason for *not* protecting it.
   The quotes on the photo may help.

4 This map shows the council's plans for the Holderness coast for the future. Suggest reasons why:
   a it does not intend to protect the whole coast
   b it will protect the coast at Bridlington
   c it will not protect the coast at X or Y
   d it will protect the coast just above Easington.

5 Draw a sketch map to show how the Holderness coast will look in 3000 AD, if the council keeps to its plans.

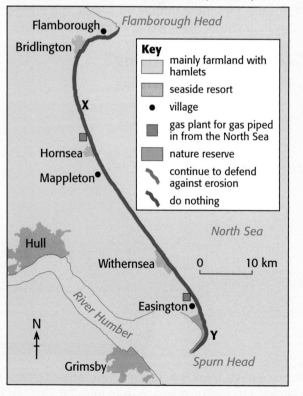

Key
- mainly farmland with hamlets
- seaside resort
- • village
- gas plant for gas piped in from the North Sea
- nature reserve
- continue to defend against erosion
- do nothing

Help! We're going under ...

Did you know?
- Britain has been tipping like a seesaw, ever since the last Ice Age.
- The north west of Scotland is rising slowly (about 3 mm a year) while the south east of England sinks.

◀ *Selsey Bill under attack by the sea. (Find it on the map below.)*

Living on an island brings its own problems!

For centuries we have fought a battle with the sea. In some places, to prevent erosion. In others, to stop the sea flooding the land. When the tide is high and the wind strong, sea floods can do a lot of damage.

But is it worth fighting on? Many people think not. Because now something even more drastic is happening – sea levels around the world are rising. That means a lot more trouble for coasts. The orange on this map shows the areas at most risk in the UK.

Why are sea levels rising?

It's all because of **global warming** …

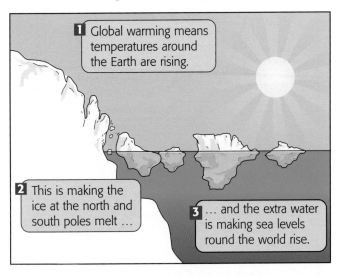

1 Global warming means temperatures around the Earth are rising.

2 This is making the ice at the north and south poles melt …

3 … and the extra water is making sea levels round the world rise.

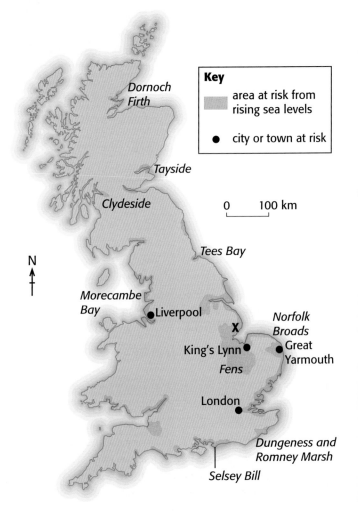

Key

area at risk from rising sea levels

● city or town at risk

Dornoch Firth

Tayside

Clydeside

0   100 km

Tees Bay

N ↑

Morecambe Bay

●Liverpool

X

Norfolk Broads

King's Lynn ●

● Great Yarmouth

Fens

London ●

Dungeness and Romney Marsh

Selsey Bill

Most scientists think we humans have caused global warming by dumping too much carbon dioxide into the air. (See page 78 for more.)

So what will become of the coast?

Global warming and rising sea levels mean …

◆ there will be more storms at sea.

◆ erosion around the coast will speed up, and many beaches and spits will get washed away.

◆ people living in unprotected areas will lose their homes and land to the sea.

◆ our existing sea walls won't be high enough to keep the sea out – so there will be more sea flooding.

◆ the flooding along the coast will drive a lot of wildlife away.

▲ *Rising sea levels means many beaches like this will be lost forever.*

Just let it flood, say MPs

A new report by a group of MPs calls for an end to our war with the sea. The report says: 'Rising sea levels threaten many of our cities. We need new sea defences to protect them. But we should give up the struggle in other places – like the farmland in South East England. We can't afford to protect everything. We should just let the sea move inland, and pay the farmers compensation.'

One gloomy estimate says sea levels could rise by at least 1 m in the next 100 years, and even up to 4 m. That would spell the end for many coastal farmers, and for landmarks like Selsey Bill.

(From a newspaper article, 6 August 1998)

Did you know?

◆ Improving our present sea defences to cope with rising sea levels would cost over £5 billion.

Did you know?

◆ Many islands will drown with rising sea levels – like Tuvalu in the Pacific (only 4 m above sea level at its highest point).

Your turn

1 Draw a simple diagram to explain why sea levels are rising.

2 To answer these questions you will need the maps on pages 20 and 121.

  a Which is the largest area at risk from rising sea levels? Explain why it's at risk.

  b Only a little of Scotland is at risk. Why?

  c Name three large cities at risk.

  d Name three seaside resorts where the beach may get washed away, as sea levels rise.

  e Name two seaside resorts that may get more crowded as a result.

3 Look at the photo on page 20. It shows the tip of Selsey Bill, a peninsula in Sussex.

  a What is a *peninsula*?

  b What protection against the sea can you see?

  c Do you think this protection will still work 100 years from now? Give your reasons.

4 This is one person's opinion. What do you think about it? Write down what you will say in reply.

We should just get on with it and build high sea walls everywhere.

5 In their report above, the members of Parliament said that coastal cities (like Liverpool) should be protected from rising sea levels. Give:

  a two *economic* reasons

  b two *social* reasons

  for protecting cities. (Glossary?)

6 Look again at the map on page 20. You have a farm at X where you grow wheat and barley.

Do you agree with the MPs? Write them a letter saying what *you* would like the government to do, and why.

What is weather?

The **weather** is the state of the atmosphere. You can tell quite a lot about it just by looking …

Thick cloud – so it will probably rain.

With all this water around, the air will feel very damp.

From the choppy sea and the spray you can tell it is windy.

No coats – so it's probably not very cold!

▲ *By the sea at Seaburn in Sunderland.*

A weather map

Now look at this map from a newspaper. It gives more details about the weather that day, in Seaburn and all over the British Isles.

It shows that the temperature in Seaburn was around 16 °C, and the wind blew from the south east at 20 miles an hour.

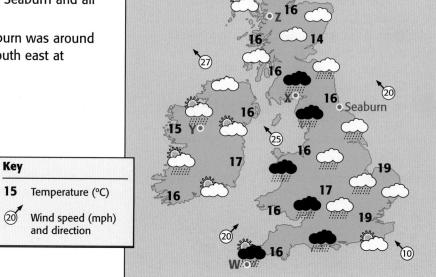

Key

15	Temperature (°C)
(20) ↗	Wind speed (mph) and direction

Your turn

A

B

1 Look at photo A above.
What was the weather like there, that day? Look for clues. Then write a list of words to describe it.
(The words in **6** might give you ideas!)

2 Now look at photo B.
 a Was it taken in the British Isles? How can you tell?
 b Imagine you were the photographer. Write a short report for your local radio, saying what the weather was like.

3 Look at the weather map on page 22.
These are symbols used on the map.
Say what each one means:

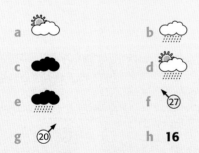

4 Find place W on the weather map.
What can you say about the weather there?
Describe it as fully as you can.

5 The weather map and photo A above are from the same day and same time. The photo was taken at one of these three places on the weather map:
X Y Z
Which one? Use the weather for clues.

6 Weather can affect our lives in a big way.
Here are some weather conditions:

hot	warm	cool	cold
frosty	freezing	icy	snowy
sunny	cloudy	dull	overcast
clear	misty	foggy	
calm	light breeze	gusty wind	gales
dry	light showers	heavy rain	cloudburst

For each activity below, choose the *two* conditions that you think would be best.

7 Now choose the two conditions you think would be *worst*, for each activity in **6**.

Measuring the weather

What's the temperature here today?

What's the air pressure?

It looks misty – so what's the visibility?

How fast is the wind blowing?

Exactly how much rain fell today?

And where's it blowing from?

How cloudy is it?

You can tell a lot about the weather just by looking. But to describe it fully …

… you need to ask questions like these. And answer them by taking measurements !

Meteorologists at work

The study of weather is called **meteorology**.
People who study weather are called **meteorologists**.

Every minute, day and night, all round the world, the weather is observed and measured. At weather stations based on land, and by equipment carried on planes, ships, weather balloons, and satellites.

The information is passed from country to country. It is fed into powerful computers, and meteorologists use it to write weather reports and make weather forecasts.

And all over the world, at home and school, people like you make their own measurements to keep track of the weather.

Did you know?
- High above us, day and night, satellites take pictures of the Earth.
- These pictures are a great help in forecasting the weather. (See page 32 for more.)

▲ They call this weather plane 'Snoopy'. Guess where the weather instruments are.

▲ A do-it-yourself weather station. The shelter is called a Stevenson screen.

Your turn

Weather term	Means ...	Usually given ...	Measured using ...
temperature	exactly how hot or cold it is		
	how 'heavy' the air is	in millibars (mb)	
	how much of the sky is hidden by clouds		your eyes; satellite image
	how fast the wind is blowing		
	where the wind is blowing from (a south west wind blows from the south west)	as a compass point (N, NW, SW and so on)	
	water falling from the sky in any form (rain, hail, sleet, snow)		
	how far ahead we can see, for example on a foggy day	in metres or kilometres	

1 This question is all about measuring the weather. You have to work out the answers for yourself, just like a detective. (The glossary will help.)

  a First, make a copy of the table above.

  b Write the words from list **A** below in the first column of your table, in the correct places.

  c Fill in the third column using list **B**. Start with the easiest units.

A Weather terms
  wind direction
  visibility
  air pressure
  precipitation
  wind speed
  cloud cover

B Units
  kilometres or miles per hour (like a car)
  millilitres
  oktas
  degrees Centigrade (°C)

2 Now look at box **C**. It shows equipment for measuring the weather. Look at each item in turn. What do you think it measures? Write its name in the correct place in the fourth column of your table.

3 **Cloud cover** means how much of the sky is covered in cloud. It is one thing you can measure just by looking. Cloud cover is measured in eighths or oktas, like this:

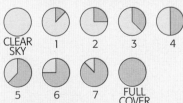

CLEAR SKY   1   2   3   4
5   6   7   FULL COVER

Note! They use more complex symbols on weather charts.

  a Now look at page 22. As far as you can tell from a photo, what do you think the cloud cover was at Seaburn that day? Answer in oktas.

  b Do the same for the top left photo on page 29.

4 a Look back at your table. Which of those aspects of the weather could you measure at home?

  b Choose one. Say *how* you would measure it, and *when*. Draw a diagram to show any equipment you'd use, and where you would place it.

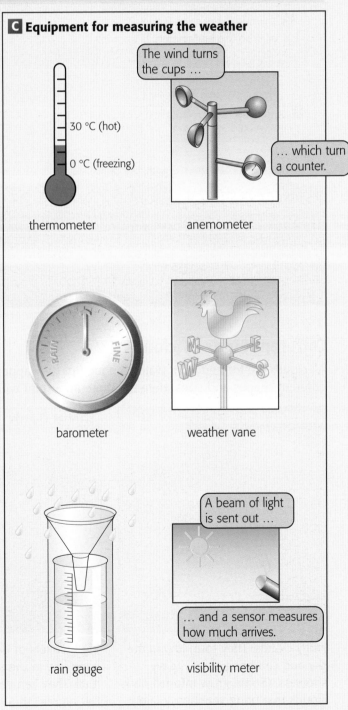

C Equipment for measuring the weather

The wind turns the cups ...
... which turn a counter.

thermometer   anemometer

30 °C (hot)
0 °C (freezing)

barometer   weather vane

A beam of light is sent out ...
... and a sensor measures how much arrives.

rain gauge   visibility meter

Clouds and rain

Look at this photo. It's 3 pm. Warm day. Blue sky. Fluffy clouds.
But there were no clouds a few hours ago. Where did they come from?

▲ *Do-it-yourself clouds!*

3 The warm air is rising.
(You just can't see it!)

4 As warm air rises it cools.
So the water vapour in it
condenses to form clouds
of tiny water droplets.

2 The ground is warming the
air – so the temperature is
rising.

5 If the water droplets
join to make larger
drops, they'll fall as rain.

1 The sun has been warming
the ground all morning.

Different kinds of clouds

All clouds are formed from water vapour. But they appear in many
different shapes and sizes. Here are three important types:

cumulus clouds

Fluffy clouds. They form low in the
sky and can bring short, heavy
showers. (Some grow into tall dark
clouds that bring very heavy rain.)

stratus clouds

Big blankets of dull cloud. They
hang low in the sky, and can cover
it all. They can give a light drizzle,
but no real showers.

cirrus clouds

Thin wispy high clouds (over 6 km
up). It's freezing up there, so they
are made of ice crystals! They can
mean bad weather is on the way.

Three types of rain

All rain is just water. All rain is caused by air rising.
But it rises for different reasons – so we give rain different names.

Convectional rainfall

Here the air rises because the ground heats it.
It rises in warm currents.
We call these **convection currents**.
So we call the rain **convectional rainfall**.

In the UK we get convectional rainfall inland in summer, where the ground gets hottest, far from the cooling effects of the sea.

3 The rising air cools.
The water vapour condenses.
Clouds form. It rains.

2 Currents of warm air rise.

1 The sun warms the ground … which then warms the air above it.

Relief rainfall

Wind is moving air.

When the wind meets a line of high hills or mountains, there's only one way to go – up!
So the air rises and cools – and we get rain.
We call it **relief rainfall**.

In the UK the prevailing wind is from the south west. So we get relief rainfall on the high land along the west coast.

3 The rising air cools. The water vapour condenses. Clouds form. It rains.

2 The air is forced to rise.

1 Warm moist air arrives from the Atlantic Ocean.

leeward (sheltered)

4 The rain falls on the **windward** side of the mountain. The **leeward** side stays dry.

windward (facing the wind)

Frontal rainfall

As you'll see in Unit 2.5, huge blocks of air called **air masses** move around the Earth.

When a warm air mass meets a cold one the warm air is forced to rise. So we get rain.
This is **frontal rainfall.**

Frontal rain can fall anywhere, since air masses can travel anywhere. But in the UK, they often arrive in from the Atlantic Ocean. So the south and west of the UK get a lot of frontal rain.

warm

2 The warm air mass slides up over the cold one, or gets driven up by it.

3 The rising air cools. The water vapour condenses. Clouds form. It rains.

1 A warm air mass meets a cold air mass.

cold

Your turn

1 Look at the clouds in the main photo on page 26.
   a Which type of clouds are they?
   b Why did they form?
   c If it rains, which kind of rainfall will this be?

2 To form clouds, two things are always needed. Which are they? Choose from this list:
   wind   rising air   mountains   hot sun
   warm ground   water vapour

3 Can clouds form in the dark? Give reasons.

4 Name a type of cloud which:
   a is made of ice crystals
   b forms a dull blanket and gives drizzle.

5 Which type of rainfall is caused by:
   a mountains in the way?
   b a mass of warm air meeting a mass of cold air?

6 Write a letter to your friend Gelop on Mars.
   Tell him what rain is, and why we humans just can't live without it.

Air pressure and weather

Although you can't feel it, the air is pressing down on the Earth. This is called **air pressure**.

Low pressure weather

Look what happens when warm air rises …

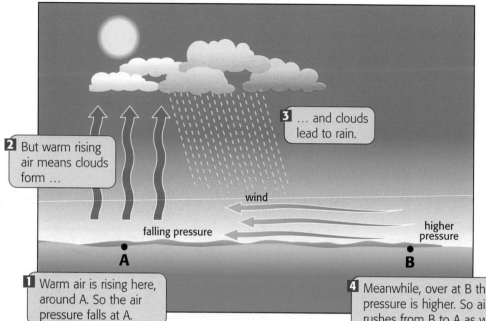

2 But warm rising air means clouds form …

3 … and clouds lead to rain.

wind

falling pressure

higher pressure

A

B

1 Warm air is rising here, around A. So the air pressure falls at A.

4 Meanwhile, over at B the air pressure is higher. So air rushes from B to A as wind.

So a fall in air pressure is a sign of rain and wind.
The lower the pressure the worse the weather will be.

High pressure weather

When warm air rises in one place, cool air sinks somewhere else.

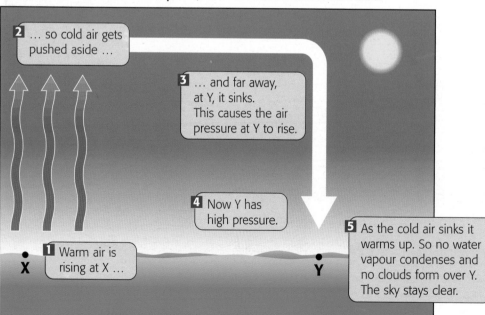

2 … so cold air gets pushed aside …

3 … and far away, at Y, it sinks. This causes the air pressure at Y to rise.

4 Now Y has high pressure.

1 Warm air is rising at X …

X

Y

5 As the cold air sinks it warms up. So no water vapour condenses and no clouds form over Y. The sky stays clear.

So high pressure means no clouds. Which means it gives us our hottest summer weather and coldest winter weather, as you'll see next.

▲ *Low pressure fashion statement.*

▲ *To see if the air pressure is rising or falling, check a barometer.*

When there's high pressure in summer ...

There are no clouds in the way so the sun is strong. Take care you don't get burned!

Since there is no cloud to trap the heat in, the evenings can be cool.

No cloud means no rain. So there may be **drought** in some places.

No cloud also means the ground gets cold at night. Water vapour condenses on grass to form **dew**.

But inland, on very hot days, the hot air may rise rapidly, cool, and form huge black clouds.

Inside these clouds, strong currents of air whip around, causing **thunderstorms** ...

... and thunderstorms can lead to heavy rain and even **flooding**.

When there's high pressure in winter ...

There is no cloud to act as a blanket. So the days are clear, cold and bright.

With no cloud, the ground cools fast at night and cools the air above it. Water vapour condenses and freezes on cold surfaces, giving **frost**.

It also condenses on dust and other particles in the air, giving **fog**. This makes driving dangerous.

Pipes may burst and homes may get flooded.

Water on roads freezes into ice as the sun goes down.

Ice and frost mean animals have trouble finding food.

Your turn

1 Write this out, using the correct word from each pair.

Low pressure is a sign of fine/unsettled weather. The lower the pressure the calmer/stormier the weather will be. High pressure brings clear/cloudy skies, which means very hot/cold weather in summer and very warm/cold weather in winter.

2 For some jobs, long spells of high pressure weather can bring problems. Try to give two examples.

3 For some jobs, long spells of low pressure weather can bring problems. Write down two examples.

4 It's August, and high pressure. You're going camping. List four items you'll pack, to cope with the weather.

5 How may high pressure affect transport in winter? (Think of boats and planes as well as cars.)

6 a What do fog, dew and frost have in common?
   b Explain how each forms.

Sudden changes in the weather

Our weather can change fast. Warm and dry one day, cool and wet the next. And all because of air masses.

Air masses

Some parts of the world are hot. Some are cold. Because of this, air is always on the move – a bit like air in a room moves when you turn on a heater.

The air moves around the world in huge blocks called **air masses**. An air mass can be thousands of km across. It can be warm or cold, damp or dry, depending on where it came from.

An air mass coming from a warm ocean will be warm and damp.

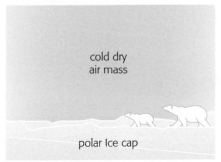

An air mass from the North Pole will be cold and dry.

▲ *Oops!*

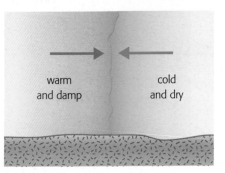

Because they are so different, when they meet …

… we get sudden changes in the weather!

Many different air masses cross Britain. That's why our weather can change so fast. But when an air mass moves very slowly, or even sits still for a while, we get the same weather for days.

Fronts

The leading edge of an air mass is called a **front**.

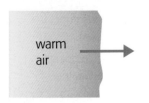

A **warm front** means a warm air mass is arriving.

On a weather map this is shown by red frills.

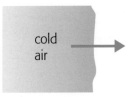

A **cold front** means a cold air mass is arriving.

On a weather map this is shown by blue teeth.

When a front arrives, it *always* brings a change in the weather.

When a warm front arrives

8 am

It's cool and dry. The sky is clear.

There's a cold air mass over your area. But a warm front is on the way.

How will it affect the weather?

midday

warm front — warm air sliding up

1 Warm air is lighter. So it slowly slides up over the cold air.
2 As it does so, the pressure falls. So it gets a bit windy.
3 The rising air cools. The water vapour condenses to form a sloping bank of cloud.
4 It starts to rain. It may rain for hours.

4 pm

Time to put away the brolly!

Now the front has passed. The warm air mass has taken over.

So the temperature has risen. The rain has eased off. The wind has dropped.

When a cold front arrives

8 am

Nice and warm – but a bit cloudy!

There's a warm air mass over your area. But a cold front is on the way.

How will it affect the weather?

midday

cold front — cold air pushing under

1 The heavy cold air advances fast. It pushes sharply under the warm air.
2 So the pressure rises sharply, causing strong gusty winds.
3 As the warm air is driven upwards, its water vapour condenses. A steep bank of thick cloud forms.
4 It rains heavily. You may even get thunderstorms.

1 pm

I wish I'd brought my coat!

The front has passed quite quickly – cold fronts travel much faster than warm ones!

Now it is cooler. The rain has stopped. The sky is clearing.

Your turn

1 What is an air mass?

2 Five main types of air mass cross Britain. This map shows where they come from. Use the letters on the arrows to answer these questions:
   a Which do you think is the coldest? Why?
   b Which three are always damp? Why?
   c Which one is very cold and dry in winter, but warmer in summer? Try to explain why.
   d Which one is warm even in winter?

3 What is: a a warm front? b a cold front?
   Draw symbols for them. Beside each symbol write *warmer* and *colder* where you think they should go.

4 It is 7 am on 16 March. There is a cold air mass in your area. A warm front will arrive about 4 pm. Write a weather forecast for your local radio.

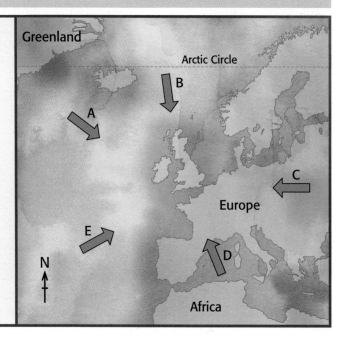

Getting the weather picture

Several times an hour, high above the Earth, satellites take pictures to help us track the weather. This is what happens:

1 Satellite cameras detect light and heat from the Earth.

2 They send signals to a computer on the Earth.

3 The computer converts the signals into images.

4 It adds country outlines. It may also add colours to make the images clearer.

5 Then we use the images to help us forecast the weather.

▲ *Taking pictures of the Earth from space.*

Example of a satellite image

This is a heat or **infrared** image showing Europe and part of Africa.
On an infrared image the *coldest* things show up *whitest*.

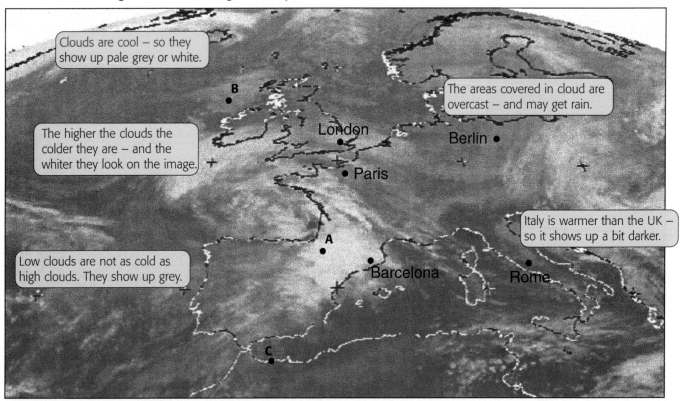

Clouds are cool – so they show up pale grey or white.

The areas covered in cloud are overcast – and may get rain.

The higher the clouds the colder they are – and the whiter they look on the image.

Low clouds are not as cold as high clouds. They show up grey.

Italy is warmer than the UK – so it shows up a bit darker.

London

Berlin •

• Paris

A

Barcelona

Rome

B

C

Satellites can detect heat even in the dark. So we can have infrared images 24 hours a day. But they can only detect light in the daytime!

Using satellite images to forecast the weather

Look at the satellite images below. (This time colour has been added.)
They show a big swirl of cloud passing over the British Isles. It's the sign
of a **depression** – a weather system where a cold front is chasing a warm
one. We get lots of depressions coming in from the Atlantic Ocean.

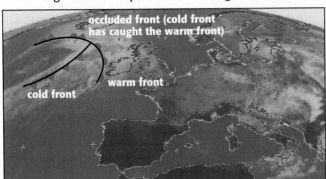

17 November, 6.30 am
The swirl of cloud shows where the cold front is
pushing under the warm air mass, forcing it to rise.

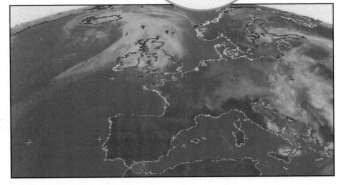

17 November, 1.30 pm
Down on the Earth, below the thick cloud, there will
be lots of rain and strong gusty winds.

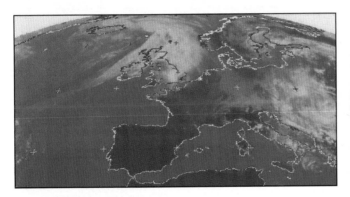

18 November, 7.00 am
The depression is moving across the UK.
The forecast warns of heavy rain and blustery
showers – especially in the south and east.

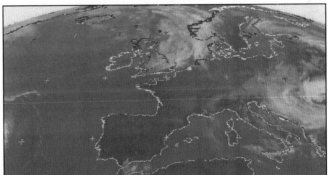

18 November, 2.30 pm
It is moving off towards Europe, where it will die
away. The forecast predicts drier weather for most
of the UK this afternoon, except the south east.

Your turn

1 Copy and complete, using words from the list below:
An _____ satellite image is made by detecting _____.
A _____ satellite image is made by detecting _____.
light   heat   infrared   visible
Questions 2–6 are about the image on page 32.

2 Where is the cloud higher, at A or at B?

3 Imagine you were on the beach at C at the time.
   a Which country is C in? (Check on page 125.)
   b Was it hot or cold at C? Sunny or cloudy?
     How can you tell from the image?

4 Which was warmer that day, the Mediterranean
   Sea or the Atlantic Ocean? How can you tell?

5 Which of the five cities had heavy cloud cover –
   perhaps 8 oktas – when the image was taken?

Answer these questions using the four images above.

6 What is a *depression*?

7 Describe the cloud shape that indicates a depression.

8 It is 17 November.
   Write a weather forecast for Radio Bristol giving
   tomorrow's weather. (Pages 121 and 31 may help.)

9 It is 1.30 pm on 17 November.
   Which of these three places do you think is having
   the worst weather?
   a London   b Belfast   c Newcastle
   Give reasons for your answer.

10 It is 18 November, 2.30 pm.
   Name two European countries that you think are
   having wet and windy weather right now.

From weather to climate

As you saw earlier, weather is the state of the atmosphere.

The weather was good when this photo was taken. But an hour later it may have been raining … because weather can change from hour to hour and day to day. Not like climate!

So what is climate?

Climate is the *average* weather in a place. It tells you what the weather is *usually* like.

It is worked out by taking weather measurements over a long period (usually 30 years) and then calculating the average.

Look at this table:

▲ *The lighthouse at Plymouth Hoe.*

Climate data for Plymouth												
Average values	Jan	Feb	Mar	Apr	May	Jun	Jul	Aug	Sep	Oct	Nov	Dec
Temperature (°C)	8	8	10	12	15	18	20	19	18	15	11	10
Rainfall (mm)	99	74	69	53	63	53	70	77	78	91	113	110
Hours of sunshine/day	1.8	2.9	4.0	6.0	7.0	7.3	6.7	6.5	5.2	3.4	2.7	1.6
Number of days with gales	3.4	1.9	1.5	0.5	0.3	0.1	0	0.3	0.9	1.3	2.2	3

Plymouth

The table shows that Plymouth is usually mild and quite wet in winter, and warm with less rain in summer. It also gets a lot more gales in winter.

Climate across the UK

Climate varies all across the UK. (You will see why in the next unit.) But we can divide the country into four climate regions.

The map on the right show the four regions. Note that:
♦ it gets colder and drier towards the east in winter
♦ the south of the UK is the warmest part.

Did you know?

♦ Fifty years from now, Plymouth could have a warmer wetter climate.
♦ That's because of global warming – see page 78.

▲ *A meteorologist working on climate data.*

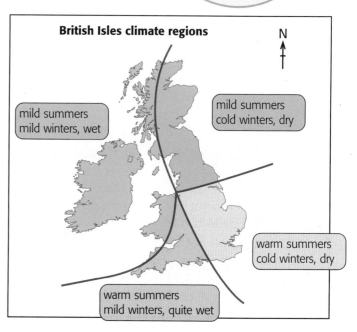

British Isles climate regions   N

mild summers mild winters, wet

mild summers cold winters, dry

warm summers cold winters, dry

warm summers mild winters, quite wet

Your turn

1 What is: **a** weather? **b** climate?

2 Look at each statement A–H below and say whether it describes weather or climate.

A It was a hot day in Boscombe when the photo on the right was taken.

B November is usually the wettest month in Plymouth.

C Egypt is usually very hot in August.

D It rained heavily all afternoon.

E May to September is the monsoon season, in South East Asia.

F In September a terrible storm carried Richard's garden shed away.

G A heavy fog on the motorway reduced visibility to less than a metre last night.

H January is a good time to head for Florida, to catch some winter sun.

3 Look at the table for Plymouth, on page 34.

a Which month usually has least sunshine?

b Which month usually gets most gales?

c Which month is usually warmest?

d Which month do *you* think would be best for a camping holiday around Plymouth? Why?

e Which do you think would be worst? Why?

4 Now look at this graph. It is a climate graph for London. It shows a bar chart and line graph together.

▲ *Boscombe in Devon, basking in the sun.*

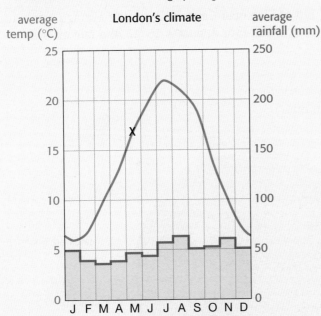

average temp (°C)   **London's climate**   average rainfall (mm)

a What does the bar chart show? (Look on the blue axis.)

b What does the line graph show? (The red axis.)

c Which month is usually hottest in London?

d Which month is usually driest?

e Which gets most rain?

5 It's your turn to draw a climate graph – for Plymouth. You will use the data from the table on page 34.

a Make a larger copy of the axes shown below, and complete the labels. (Use graph paper if you can, and make each axis a different colour.)

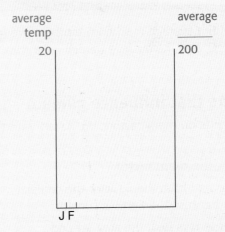
average temp   average _____

b Now draw in a bar chart showing rainfall for Plymouth. Check the bar chart for London, to see how to do it.

c Next draw in a line graph for the temperature. Mark each point at the centre of the month (like the X for May, for London). Join the points with a smooth curve.

d Give your graph a title.

6 Compare the climate graphs for London and Plymouth. Which of the two places:

a gets more rain?   **b** is hotter in summer?

c is colder in winter?

See if you can come up with a reason for each answer.

The factors that influence climate

Climate is the average weather in a place. It's what the weather *is usually* like there. It can be very different in different places. For example …

… in London the average maximum temperature for August is 21 °C, and the average rainfall is 59 mm.

But at Giza near Cairo in Egypt, the average maximum temperature for August is 35 °C. And rainfall is zero!

The factors that influence climate

Climate depends on many factors. We'll start with the main one.

1 Latitude – the main factor

The further you go from the equator the cooler it gets. That's because the Earth is curved.

Look at A. These rays heat the area around the equator. The Earth gets hottest here.

Now look at B. Because the Earth is curved, these rays are spread over a larger area of the Earth – so it gets less hot.

C covers an even larger area – which hardly even gets warm!

So that is why:

◆ the UK is always cooler than Egypt.

◆ the north of the UK is usually cooler than the south.

◆ it is very cold at the North and South Poles.

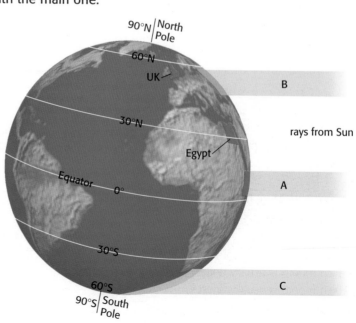

2 Other general factors

Distance from the coast
The sea is cooler than land in summer, and warmer in winter. So a sea breeze keeps the coast cool in summer – and warm in winter!

Prevailing wind direction
For example in the UK the prevailing wind is from the south west. It brings water vapour from the ocean – and that means rain!

Ocean currents
For example a warm ocean current called the North Atlantic Drift warms the west coast of the UK in winter, by warming the wind.

3 Local factors

Even places close together can have different climates, due to these factors:

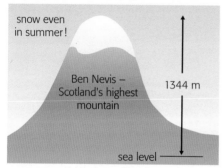

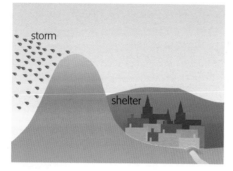

Height above sea level
Or **altitude**. The higher you are above sea level, the cooler it is. The temperature falls by about 1 °C for every 100 metres.

Shelter
One place may be warm and dry because it is sheltered by hills. Another may be exposed to the wind and rain.

How built up a place is
Roofs and streets store up heat. Cars and central heating give out heat. So the city tends to be warmer than the countryside.

Your turn

1 Draw a spider map to show the factors that influence climate. Make it look interesting!
You could use a symbol for each factor, and a different colour for each group of factors.

2 Using the map on page 121, give *two* reasons why:
 a Aberdeen is colder than Plymouth in winter
 b it's always colder up Ben Nevis than in Plymouth
 c London is warmer than Belfast in summer.

3 In the UK, the *prevailing wind* is a south west wind.
 a What does this mean? (Glossary!)
 b Explain how this wind affects the climate.

4 Suppose the prevailing wind in the UK was a north wind. How do you think this would affect the climate?

5 This is about the effect of distance from the coast.

In an oven, soil heats up faster than water. When you take them out of the oven, the soil cools faster too. Using this idea, and the map on page 125, explain why:
 a Tehran is hotter than Lisbon in summer
 b Lisbon is warmer than Tehran in winter.

6 Now design and draw a diagram to explain why it is warmer by the coast in winter than inland.

7 Here's a challenge! Try to explain why it gets colder as you go up a mountain.

Climate across Europe

Europe, the continent you live on. 10 million square kilometres …

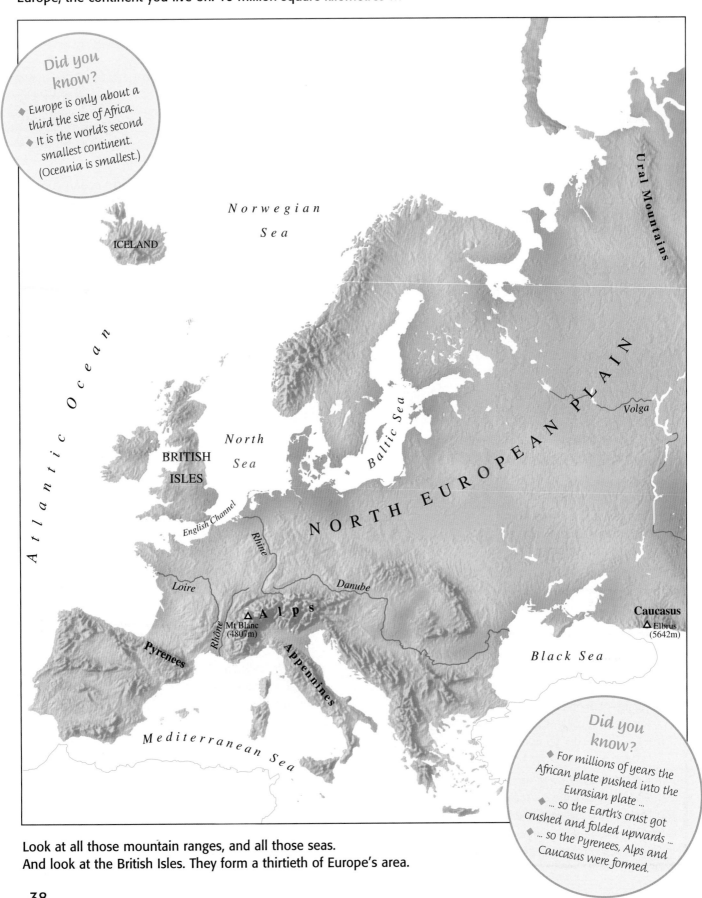

Did you know?

◆ Europe is only about a third the size of Africa.
◆ It is the world's second smallest continent. (Oceania is smallest.)

Norwegian Sea

ICELAND

Atlantic Ocean

North Sea

BRITISH ISLES

English Channel

Ural Mountains

Baltic Sea

Volga

NORTH EUROPEAN PLAIN

Rhine

Loire

Danube

Rhône △ **Alps**
Mt Blanc (4807m)

Pyrenees

Appennines

Caucasus
△ Elbrus (5642m)

Black Sea

Mediterranean Sea

Did you know?

◆ For millions of years the African plate pushed into the Eurasian plate …
◆ … so the Earth's crust got crushed and folded upwards …
◆ … so the Pyrenees, Alps and Caucasus were formed.

Look at all those mountain ranges, and all those seas.
And look at the British Isles. They form a thirtieth of Europe's area.

Climate across Europe

This map shows Europe's **climate zones**.
Note the general pattern:

◆ Europe gets warmer towards the south.

◆ It gets drier towards the east.

◆ The prevailing wind blows in from the Atlantic Ocean. (But other winds blow in too – for example from the North Pole and from Africa.)

◆ The change from hot summer to cold winter is greatest in eastern Europe.

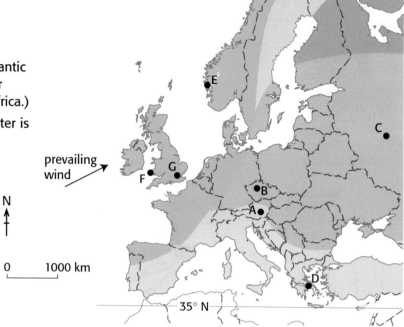

Key

▨	mild winters, cool summers, rain all year (west coast maritime)
▨	mild wet winters, hot dry summers (Mediterranean)
▨	cold winters with snow, warm summers with showers (Alpine mountain)
▨	cold dry winters, hot damp summers (continental)
▨	cold all year, little rain (tundra)

Your turn

Now you are about to become a detective, and work out *why* Europe's climate varies the way it does. You will use what you learned in Unit 2.8.

1 The map opposite is a *physical* map of Europe. The one on page 122 is a *political* map. Explain what the difference is.

2 Use both maps to help you answer these.
  a Name the mountain range on the borders of France and Spain.
  b Name the mountain range that shelters Italy from cold north winds, and four countries it goes through.
  c Which country has Europe's highest mountain?
  d What is a plain? Name the largest plain in Europe.

3 Now look at the map of climate zones above.
  a To which climate zone does the UK belong?
  b Explain why this climate zone has mild winters.
  c Give a reason why it has quite a lot of rain.
  d Name four other countries with a climate like ours.

4 a Name Europe's most southern climate zone.
  b Why is it called this?
  c Give one reason why it is hotter than the west coast maritime zone in summer.
  d In summer this area often has high pressure. What effect does this have on the climate?
  e This zone gets rain in winter, but not as much as the UK does. Suggest a reason.

5 Three areas on the map have an Alpine climate. Explain why, for each of them. (Page 38 will help.)

6 Look at the places marked on the climate map. Suggest reasons why:
  a A is always cooler than B even though it is further south.
  b C gets quite hot in summer and very cold in winter.
  c B gets mainly convectional rain in summer.
  d D is very hot and dry in summer.
  e E gets a lot of relief rain.
  f F gets more rain than G.

7 Now look at these climate graphs. Your job is to match them to A, B, C and D on the climate map. Give your answer like this: ① = ___.

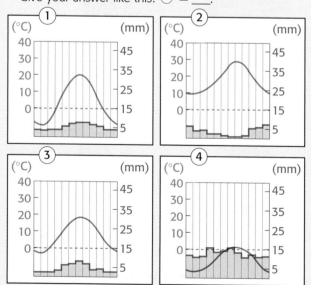

How climate affects our lives

Climate affects our lives in all kinds of ways.
For example when we are deciding …

… what to wear …   … where to go on holiday …

… what to eat …   … what to do in our free time.

Here again is the map of climate zones in Europe.
Now you will investigate some of the ways that
climate affects our lives.

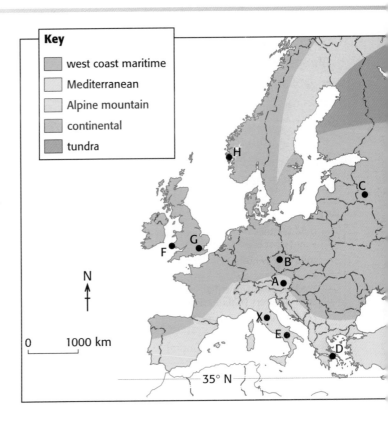

Key

	west coast maritime
	Mediterranean
	Alpine mountain
	continental
	tundra

N

0   1000 km

35° N

Your turn

1 Here are four things you could do on holiday.
Match them to four of the seven places A–G
marked on the map above.

i   in September

ii   in April

iii   in February

iv   in November

Give your answer like this: **i =**

2 Now look at these two houses.

i

ii

Match each house to one of the four places
A, D, E, F, marked on the map above.
Then explain how it suits the climate there.

Orange trees suit high areas with cool dry winters and warm wet summers. Frost and drought can kill them.

Wheat can grow in a wide range of climates. But it does best in hot summers with frequent light showers.

Cotton grows best in a warm climate with at least 150 frost-free days. It needs water – but not lots of rain.

Warm summers with lots of sunshine and not much rain are best for grapes. Frost in spring can ruin the harvest.

3 Look at the crops above, and the conditions they need.

a Which of these would be best for growing oranges?
UK   Poland   Spain

b Which of these climate zones would suit grapes best?
west coast maritime   tundra   Mediterranean

c One of these countries grows quite a lot of cotton. Which one do you think it is?
Norway   Greece   Ukraine

d One of these countries is among the world's top wheat producers. Which do you think it is?
Russia   Greece   Iceland

4 Look at the six events on the right. They took place in a village called Porziano in Italy. (It's at X on the map on page 40.) Each event is linked to the climate.

Climate graph for Porziano

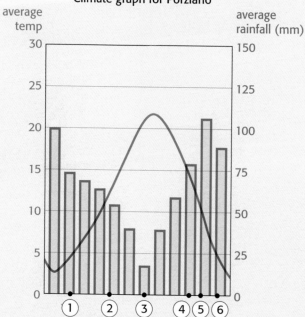

average temp

average rainfall (mm)

Your task is to match each event to one of the numbers ① – ⑥ on the climate graph.
Answer like this: ① = ___

This one's for below 15 °C.

Always I do zis in the driest month.

a Georgio puts on his special jumper, for the first time since spring.

b The mayor sends out his annual letter asking people to save water.

At 5 above freezing, stew is so pleezing.

Mamma mia! É orribilé at this time of year.

c At Sergio's, lamb stew goes on the menu once again.

d Maria greets last month's electricity bill with horror.

For you, carote mie bellissime!

Ecco! They always sell best this month.

e Uncle Paulo starts to water his carrots. They need at least 60 mm of water a month.

f At the door of her shop, Alice puts out a tub of umbrellas.

What is an ecosystem?

The wood on the right looks so quiet and peaceful.
But don't be fooled – it is bursting with action!
Below are just *some* of the things going on …

A robin snacks on a crispy spider.

A caterpillar feeds on a crunchy leaf.

Millions of leaves are busy making food from air and water – with sunlight as fuel.

A squirrel considers. Eat the nut now, or hide away for later?

A fox munches on a woodmouse – a treat! It had earthworm and caterpillar for starters.

A wood mouse chews on a caterpillar.

The mushrooms feed silently on dead wood.

A blackbird tugs at its wriggling lunch.

An earthworm drags a leaf home to its larder.

A woodlouse dines on a dead leaf.

Millions of roots are busy taking in water and minerals from the soil.

In the soil, billions of bacteria are busy feeding on dead things. Yummy!

It's an ecosystem

The wood on page 42 is an **ecosystem**. An ecosystem is made up of two parts:

◆ living things (plants, animals, bacteria) and
◆ their non-living surroundings or **environment** – air, water, soil and the climate (how warm or wet it is).

The living things interact with the environment and each other. For example caterpillars breathe the air. They feed on leaves, and get eaten by birds. If it gets too cold they die.

Did you know?
◆ *Insects, birds and fish are all animals.*
◆ *Grass and trees are plants.*
◆ *Mushrooms are fungi – a special type of plant.*

Did you know?
◆ *Bacteria are not plants or animals. They form a kingdom of their own.*

How big is an ecosystem?

An ecosystem is any size you choose to study. For example:

a pond   a meadow   a forest   the Sahara desert   the whole Earth

Each is made up of living things and a non-living environment.

Your turn

1 This shows part of the ecosystem from page 42.

air ———— tree
                                    fox
              mushroom
water
        caterpillar
                              earthworm
soil
              wood mouse
warmth   bacteria

a A line links *tree* and *air*. What do you think the line means?
b *Caterpillar* and *warmth* are also linked. Why?
c Copy the diagram. If you can, write each of these four groups in a different colour:
  plants   animals   bacteria
  non-living parts of the environment
d Now draw lines to link items, where you think one interacts with the other. Try to use a fifth colour for your lines. You will end up with a lot of lines. Don't worry if they cross words and each other.

2 Woodland changes all through the year. The photo on page 42 shows it in summer.
  a Name one way the non-living environment will change as winter draws near.
  b How will this affect the trees?
  c How will it affect squirrels? What will they do?
3 Is this an ecosystem? Explain your answer.

a an ocean

b a jungle

Moi?

c a goldfish in a bowl

Feeding in an ecosystem

An ecosystem is like a canteen, where you choose your favourite foods!

It all starts with plants …

Plants are really smart. They do something no other living things can do. They *make their own food inside themselves*. They use the sun's energy for this – just like we use electricity for cooking.

1 The plant traps the sun's energy in **chlorophyll**, the green stuff in leaves.

2 It takes in **carbon dioxide** through its leaves, and **water** through its roots.

3 It uses the sun's energy to turn these into **glucose**. The process is called **photosynthesis**.

4 It combines glucose with minerals from the soil to make all the things it needs to grow.

The minerals it needs are called **nutrients**. They include nitrogen, potassium and phosphorus.

Did you know?
- A few plants can feed on insects.
- They trap the insects in a tiny bowl of liquid that just dissolves them away.

What happens next?

Let's take a plant in the wood as an example.

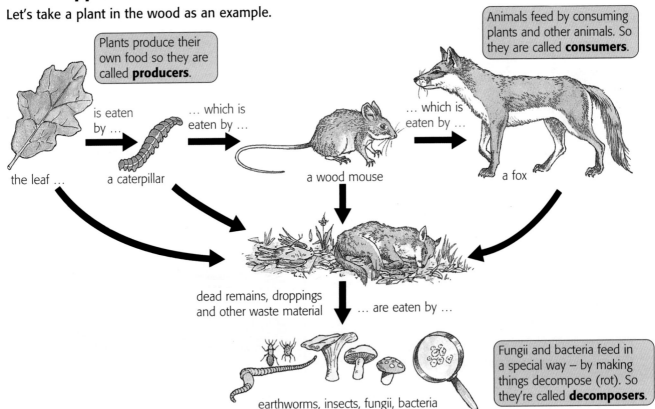

Plants produce their own food so they are called **producers**.

Animals feed by consuming plants and other animals. So they are called **consumers**.

the leaf …   is eaten by …   a caterpillar   … which is eaten by …   a wood mouse   … which is eaten by …   a fox

dead remains, droppings and other waste material   … are eaten by …

earthworms, insects, fungii, bacteria

Fungii and bacteria feed in a special way – by making things decompose (rot). So they're called **decomposers**.

It's the same in *every* ecosystem.

- The plants make their own food – and then get eaten.
- There are always things to eat up dead and waste material.
- Without the plants, all the other living things would die.

Food chains

This is a **food chain**. It shows what eats what. The arrow means *eaten by*.

plant ⟶ caterpillar ⟶ wood mouse ⟶ fox

A food chain always starts with a plant. The energy from the sun, which was trapped by the plant, is passed along the chain. That means the sun is the real source of energy for all living things.

Food webs

Often several consumers feed on the same thing. For example both caterpillars and aphids (a type of fly) feed on oak leaves.

So food chains link to form a **food web**. This diagram shows just part of the food web for an oak wood.

The complete food web for the wood is very large and complex.

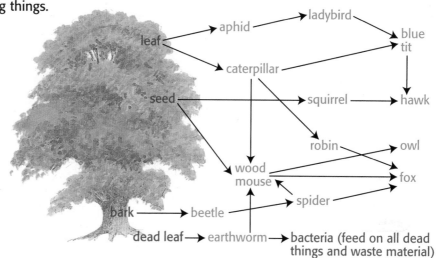

The recyclers

In the end, every living thing in an ecosystem dies, and becomes a feast for the decomposers. And they do a really important job: they **recycle**.

When they make material rot, they release the nutrients from it. These sink back into the soil and get used all over again, as this diagram shows. Without decomposers the soil would very quickly run out of nutrients. So no plants would grow, and ecosystems would collapse.

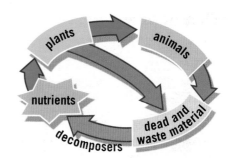

Your turn

1 Copy and complete, choosing words from page 44. Plants are called _____ because they make their own food. They start with _____ _____ and water. Animals are called _____ because they obtain food by eating _____ and other _____. Bacteria in the soil are called _____ because they make dead material rot away.

2 Name:
   a a producer found in the school playing field
   b a consumer that is also a farm animal
   c a decomposer that gets put on pizzas!

3 Look at the photo on the right.
   a What animal does it show?
   b Is it a producer, consumer or decomposer?
   c What will happen to the nutrients in the leaf? Is this a good thing or a bad thing? Give reasons.

4 Look at the food web above. What would suffer if:
   a a disease wiped out all the aphids in a wood?
   b all the trees in the wood got chopped down?

5 Look again at the food web. If all the foxes were wiped out:
   a what might happen to the number of wood mice?
   b what else could happen because of the change in a?

6 'All ecosystems depend on the sun.' Do you agree? Draw a diagram to help you explain your answer.

Down with lunch.

Where do humans fit in?

The Earth is the largest ecosystem of all, and we humans are part of it. But we are not like the other animals. We try to **control** and **manage** what's around us.

Once upon a time

At first, our ancestors lived by hunting, and eating seeds, nuts, berries and insects. Just like other animals. They moved around …

… in search of food. But then, one day, they made a great discovery. Where they dropped seeds, new plants grew. Amazing!

From then on, their lives began to change. They became farmers. They sowed seeds to get crops, and kept live animals as a food store.

They had started to manage their ecosystems. Now they didn't need to move around searching for food. They could settle in one place.

Then along came another smart idea. If they produced more food than they needed, they could swap it for other things.

Today, our farmers still produce food – and swap it for money. Most of it gets frozen or cooked or packaged before you buy it.

Humans in the food chain

So this is where *we* fit in the food chain:

Did you know?
- Our ancestors ate termites and other insects.
- They dug the termites from their mounds using bones. (Find the termite mound on page 102.)

How we affect the Earth's ecosystems

10 000 years ago there were about 4 million humans on the Earth.

Today there are over 6000 million of us (6 billion) and we have spread over most of the Earth.

We are clever and inventive, and always looking for ways to improve our standard of living. But at the same time we damage many ecosystems, as this photo shows.

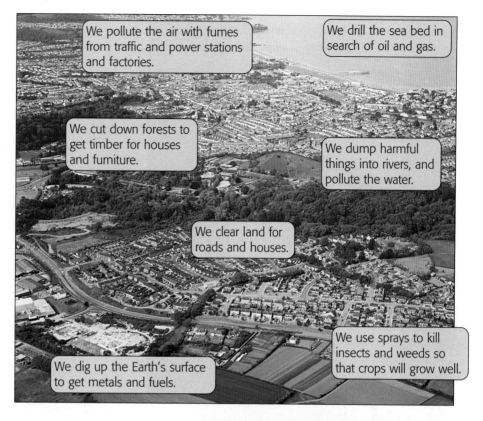

We pollute the air with fumes from traffic and power stations and factories.

We drill the sea bed in search of oil and gas.

We cut down forests to get timber for houses and furniture.

We dump harmful things into rivers, and pollute the water.

We clear land for roads and houses.

We dig up the Earth's surface to get metals and fuels.

We use sprays to kill insects and weeds so that crops will grow well.

Did you know?

◆ On average, 130 species of plants and animals become extinct each day.

We kill off plants and animals when we destroy their environments. Every year, thousands of different **species** (kinds) of plants and animals disappear for ever. They become **extinct**. And when one species goes, the rest of its food web suffers.

It does not have to be like this …

We need houses and roads and fuel and food. But we can get what we need *without* destroying other species, or wasting things. That is called **sustainable living**.
You will see examples later in this book.

▲ *Happy – and almost extinct.*

Your turn

1 a Name a meal you like. (Fish nuggets and chips?)
  b Now draw the food chain for it, like the one at the bottom of page 46 or at the top of page 45.
  c That meal gives you energy. On your diagram show how the energy gets into the food and is passed along to you.

2 Look at these definitions:
    a **herbivore** eats only plants
    a **carnivore** eats only animals
    an **omnivore** eats both plants and animals

  a Give two examples of herbivores.
  b Give two examples of carnivores.
  c Which term describes most humans?

3 List 4 ways we humans damage ecosystems.
4 These drawings show one way we kill off birds. But they're all mixed up.

  a Redraw them in the correct order. (You don't have to copy them exactly. Keep your drawing simple.)
  b Now write a short caption under each drawing to explain what's happening – not more that 8 words.

The Earth's main ecosystems

You can divide the Earth into eight *huge* ecosystems or **biomes**. Each has its own type of plants or **vegetation**. Here are four of the biomes …

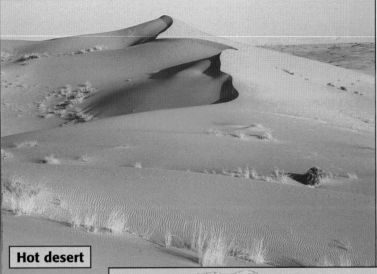

Hot desert

Tropical rainforest

Deciduous forest

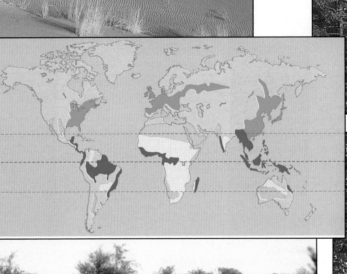

Savanna

The UK belongs to the deciduous forest biome. **Deciduous** means the trees lose their leaves in winter. Most trees in the UK are like this.

5000 years ago, most of the UK was covered in great deciduous forests. It would still be like that if no-one lived here. But over the centuries we humans have cut down the forests for wood and fuel, and to make way for farms and villages and towns. Now there are not many forests left.

The woodland on page 42 is the remains of a large forest.

Why are they so different?

The ecosystems on the last page have very different vegetation – mainly because they have very different climates!

1 the soil
How thick and rich the soil is depends partly on the climate. Rock breaks down fastest into soil in a hot damp climate.

which affects …

The climate
The climate is the main driving force in an ecosystem. It affects …

2 the vegetation
It has developed or **adapted** to suit the climate and soil. Plants grow fastest and thickest in a hot damp sunny climate.

which affects …

3 the animals
They have adapted to feed on the plants or each other, and cope with the climate.

In the next unit you'll see how this works.

Your turn

1 a Make a table like the one started here, for the four ecosystems shown on page 48.

Ecosystem	What is the climate like?
hot desert	

b Write their names in the first column – in order of temperature. Start with the one that gets hottest. The climate graphs on the right will help.

c Write these descriptions in the correct places in the second column. (Check the climate graphs.)

> Hot. Quite a lot of rain – but has a dry season with little or no rain.

> Very hot in some months, much cooler in others. Hardly any rain.

> Hot and wet all year. The temperature does not vary much. In some months the rain is really heavy.

> Never gets very hot. Rains quite a bit all through the year.

2 Now use the photos on page 48 and your table for question 1 to help you answer these questions.

a Which ecosystem has least vegetation? Why is this?

b Which has the tallest thickest vegetation? Why?

c The vegetation in the savanna gets all dried out for part of the year. Why is this?

d Deciduous forests lose their leaves in winter. Why?

e The rainforest stays green all year. Why?

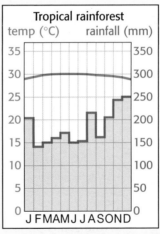

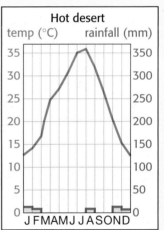

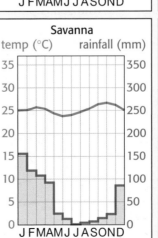

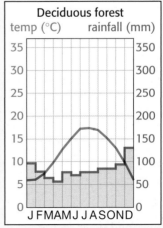

The tropical rainforests

The tropical rainforests are in the tropics, where it's hot and wet all year. So let's see how the vegetation has adapted to the climate.

What about me?

Hey, look at me!

Where did that one emerge from?

It's about 140 million years ago. The tropical rainforests are just starting to grow.

Plants grow well in the damp heat – so well that soon they have to fight for sunlight.

One way to win is to grow tall and straight. But that's not the only way. For example …

Let's loop to the light.

Just perching.

no flowers, to save energy

large leaves, green all year, to trap as much light as possible

… thick vines called **lianas** just loop around tree trunks to reach sunlight.

Air plants or **epiphytes** forget about roots, and perch up high on branches.

Species like **ferns** solved the problem by adapting to life in the shade.

The warmer and damper the faster we work!

I'm no pushover!

On the ground, insects munch. And bacteria work fast, releasing nutrients from all waste material.

The soil is poor. So the plant roots grow close to the surface, to grab these nutrients.

The tallest trees have developed huge **buttress roots** like these, to stop them toppling over.

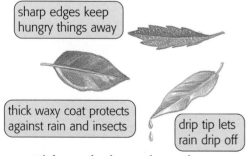

sharp edges keep hungry things away

thick waxy coat protects against rain and insects

drip tip lets rain drip off

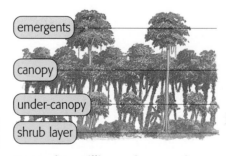

emergents

canopy

under-canopy

shrub layer

High up, the leaves have also developed ways to protect themselves.

Now, after millions of years of growth, the vegetation in the rainforest forms four layers …

The canopy is the thickest layer. So most of the animals and insects have adapted to living there.

Why the rainforests are our richest ecosystem

For millions of years the rainforests lay undisturbed. Small tribes of humans lived there – but did no damage. They fished and hunted and picked fruit and nuts to eat.

So the plants and animals were able to develop and adapt in peace. And that's why the rainforests now have *thousands* of different kinds of plants and animals. Look at these two examples:

Some rainforest trees
mahogany
ebony
palm
rubber
banana

Some rainforest animals
apes
parrots
sloths
jaguars
pythons
alligators

Did you know?
- The rainforests cover 6% of the Earth's surface.
- But they are home to over half its species.

The tree frog. The pads on its fingers and toes help it to grasp branches. It climbs high in the canopy to get all that nice rain.

The sloth. Its strong claws allow it to hang from branches. Its hair is filled with green algae (tiny plants) to help it hide among the leaves.

Your turn

1 A two-storey house is about 5 metres tall.

This table shows the heights of the layers in the rainforest.

Layer	Height (m)
1	35–60
2 canopy	20–30
3	3–5
4	less than 1

a Make a larger copy of this diagram.

b Draw in the four layers on your diagram, at the correct heights, and name them.

c Give your diagram a title.

d *The tallest emergent is __ times as tall as the house.* What's the missing number?

2 Copy and complete these statements.

a Most insects and animals in the rainforest live in the canopy, because …

b Many leaves have drip tips so that …

c Roots grow close to the soil surface so that …

d The emergents have buttress roots so that …

e The plants on the forest floor have dark green leaves all year round so that …

3

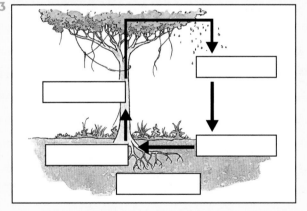

This drawing shows part of rainforest. Make a large copy of it, and add these labels in the correct boxes.

The roots quickly take up the nutrients again.

Decomposers release the nutrients from them.

The nutrients help the vegetation to grow.

Dead leaves and animal waste fall all year round.

The soil down here is poor because the nutrients don't get a chance to sink in.

What are we doing to the rainforests?

The Earth's rainforests flourished for millions of years.
But in the last 50 years, we have destroyed over half of them.

1 The main reason is to clear the land for farming – usually by burning the trees down.

I came here to build a big cattle ranch.

All that lovely beef for hamburgers.

We came here from town because we're so poor. We're just clearing a patch of land to grow food.

Otherwise we will starve!

2 **Logging** is also a culprit.

People want hard woods like mahogany and teak, for building and making furniture.

We have to chop down nearly 30 trees to find 1 hardwood tree!

We have permission from the government.

I haven't! But the rainforest is so big they won't catch me.

3 Companies exploring for **oil** and **metal** add to the problem …

We're drilling a hole to search for oil …

… and we're looking for gold and copper.

4 Government plans don't always help.

We need a motorway to the coast.

Let's just run it through here.

It will be great for business.

5 Local tribes suffer.

Our people have lived here for thousands of years.

We treat the rainforest with respect.

But now outsiders are taking our land away.

When we refused to go, they even tried to kill us!

6 The animals suffer.

They destroy the plants we eat and the trees we live in.

Roads scare us away …

… and make it easy for hunters to reach us!

7 The soil suffers.

When the trees are cleared the soil quickly becomes useless …

… because the heavy rain washes the nutrients away – and there are no dead leaves to make more.

8 You suffer!

Millions of species are being killed off for ever …

… including plants that could cure diseases.

And burning the forest produces carbon dioxide …

… which speeds up global warming!

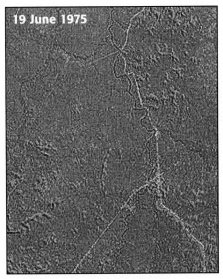

19 June 1975

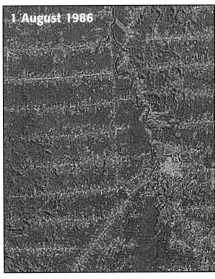

1 August 1986

22 June 1992

▲ *Satellite images of the Brazilian rainforest. Red shows living trees. White shows where they've been cut down.*

Your turn

1 Look at the three photos above.
   a Describe the changes you see.
   b Who do you think was responsible for them?
   c List all the groups who will suffer because of the changes. (Wildlife is one!)

2 Much of the rainforest is destroyed by burning.

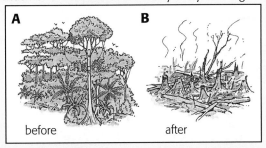

A   B

before   after

The soil in B will soon be useless. Give at least two reasons for this.

3 'People living far from the rainforest help to destroy it.' Is that true? Explain your answer.

4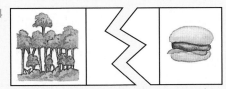

Draw a strip cartoon like this one to show how a hamburger may be linked to the destruction of the rainforest. You can show up to 7 boxes.

5 Look at the photo on the right.
   a What is going on here?
   b Who do you think the people are?
   c What do they mean by 'Mahogany is murder'?
   d How could this event help to save the rainforest ecosystem?

6 All around the world rainforests are being destroyed. Here are some opinions about this:

a The rainforests belong to the whole human race, so we must look after them.

c It's okay for you – but we're a poor country. We need to make as much money as we can from our rainforest.

b You people in Europe have cut down most of your forests. So why shouldn't we?

Write down what *you* think about each of these points of view.

The savanna

The savanna biome covers about a quarter of the land on the Earth. The largest area of savanna is in Africa. Look at this map.

The effect of the climate

You saw earlier that vegetation grows best in warm damp places.

♦ In the savanna it is warm to hot all year (20–35 °C).

♦ Some parts get quite a lot of rain. Others get only a little.

♦ But there is one big problem. Most of the rain falls in just a few months – the **wet season**. There is hardly any the rest of the year. The vegetation and animals (and people) have had to adapt to this.

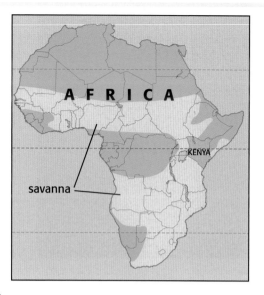

In the wet season

This shows the savanna in Kenya, in the wet season. (Look at the map.)

The vegetation springs to life in the wet season. It's the **growing season**.

Since there is plenty of space and plenty of vegetation to eat, there are lots of large animals.

In fact there are over 40 species of herbivore, including zebra, gazelles and wildebeest.

There are not many trees – because trees need a lot of water.

Giraffes have developed long necks to feed on acacia leaves.

Many have adapted to travelling long distances – to look for grass in the dry season.

The trees that do grow here have adapted to survive drought.

Other animals like lions, hyenas and cheetahs have adapted to feed on them!

Bushes have thorns instead of leaves, to prevent water loss and protect them from animals.

For example the **acacia tree** has small leaves covered with wax, to cut down water loss.

The grass grows fast – and up to 3 m tall.

The soil gets soaked in the wet season – and baked in the dry season. So a brick-hard layer forms below the surface.

It has long **tap roots** to reach moisture in the dry season.

The hard layer stops roots pushing down into the soil. (So trees can only grow where there are cracks in it.)

In the dry season

This is the same savanna, in the dry season.

The trees have lost their leaves, to prevent water loss.

The **baobab tree** stored water in its huge trunk in the wet season. That will help it survive now.

The grass has turned brown and died down.

The thick bark of the baobab and acacia help them to withstand fire. (There are many fires in the dry season.)

Nothing left to eat – so the large animals have moved away.

▲ Burning the savanna. The ash makes the soil more fertile for next season.

▲ Wildebeest – strong shoulders and long legs help them travel long distances.

Your turn

1 Name:
   a two producers   b six consumers
   c two carnivores   d three herbivores
   that are found in the African savanna.

2 This sketch shows an acacia tree and a baobab tree. Make a larger copy. Then add labels to show how each has adapted to the climate.

3 Give two ways in which the wildebeest has adapted to the savanna ecosystem.

4 The farmers of the savanna are mostly **pastoralists**.
   a What does that mean? (Try the glossary.)
   b Why do you think they became pastoralists?

5 Explain why the farmers:
   a often have to walk a long way with their herds
   b set the savanna on fire in the dry season
   c often find it difficult to plough the soil.

6 Now look at the climate graph for a savanna region, on page 49.
   a The dry season never has more than 30 mm of rain a month, and usually much less. How long is it?
   b What problems will this cause for the farmers?
   c What problems will it cause for their families?

Farming in the fragile savanna

Farmers need good soil. But the soil in the
savanna is fragile, and easily ruined. Like this …

1 A place in the African savanna. Trees,
grass, wild animals. Sometimes farmers
bring their herds here to graze.

2 Now your tribe starts to settle here.

◆ You drive the wild animals away.
◆ You chop trees down to build huts,
and for firewood.
◆ You clear the land to grow crops.
◆ When the soil in one patch gets too
hard or worn out, you just move to
another.

3 The population is growing fast.
There are farms everywhere, and cattle
grazing everywhere. And soon …

◆ there is no new land to move to. So
you stay on the same old patch.
◆ the soil is getting worn out because
the crops are taking all its nutrients.
You don't know what to do.
◆ your herd is eating up every blade of
grass, so the ground is bare and
trampled.
◆ most of the trees are gone. You have
to walk miles for firewood.

4 Now …

◆ Your soil has lost all its goodness.
It is turning to dust.
◆ There are no trees or grass to protect it.
◆ So it gets blown away by the wind in
the dry season, and washed away by
the rain in the wet season.

You are left with a rock-hard patch of
ground. How can you feed your family?

> **Did you know?**
> ◆ Millions of hectares of savanna have been ruined by human activity.
> ◆ Millions of people are suffering as a result.

▲ *Eat up all the grass, and the soil gets blown away.*

The soil problem

Look at these two photos. The ground is no longer much good for growing crops. This is a problem in many parts of the savanna.

Sometimes the rain fails too. So drought kills any crops you *do* grow. That can mean famine.

But the good news is – it doesn't have to be that way. You can find out more in the next unit.

▲ *Heavy rain on bare worn-out soil caused this big gash or* **gully***. They can't grow any crops here now.*

Your turn

1 All of these affect the soil in the savanna:

  a the climate   b human activity   c animals

Explain how each of them can help to destroy the soil. You could draw pictures for your answers.

2 a Make a large copy of this diagram.

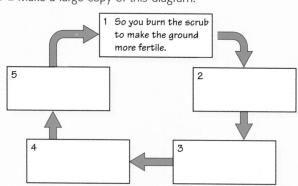

b Now write these statements in the correct boxes, to show how the soil can get worse and worse.

So your crops grow poorer and poorer.

So more gets blown or washed away.

So more soil gets baked to dust.

But your family needs food or it will starve.

3 The photo on the right above shows a gully. This drawing shows how a gully begins to form.

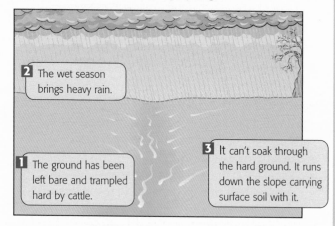

2 The wet season brings heavy rain.

1 The ground has been left bare and trampled hard by cattle.

3 It can't soak through the hard ground. It runs down the slope carrying surface soil with it.

You are a farmer in the savanna. What could you do to stop gullies developing? Try to give several suggestions.

The Machakos miracle

Soil can be a matter of life and death.
These photos show a place called Machakos in the savanna in Kenya.

1937. The soil is worn out and eroded. A soil inspector wrote:
*The land is turning into a desert of rocks, stones and sand.
And the people are drifting into hopeless poverty.*

1987. The soil is in much better shape. There is no sign of erosion. Now there are more trees, more crops – and more people! They call it the Machakos miracle.

The people of Machakos are not rich. They have no electricity, poor roads and not enough wells. But they have learned to live **sustainably** in the savanna. Study the next page before you answer these questions.

Your turn

1

How the population of Machakos has grown		
Year	1930	1987
Population	240 000	1 320 000

a How many times larger was the population in 1987 than in 1930?

b A rise in population *could* make soil worse. Explain why. (Page 56 will help.)

2 List all the steps the Machakos farmers took, to:
a prevent soil erosion b improve soil quality
c conserve trees.

3 Look at the bar chart on the right. *Output* means the amount produced. For example of maize.
a About how many times larger was the total output in 1987 than in 1930?
b Output fell in 1961. Suggest a reason.
c Give one cash crop grown in Machakos. (Glossary?)
d What happened to the output of cash crops between 1961 and 1987? Give a reason.
e Which output didn't change much over the years?

f What do you think *food crops* are? Name one food crop grown in Machakos.

g Which type of output grew fastest between 1977 and 1987?

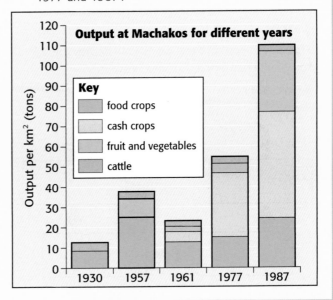

Output at Machakos for different years

Output per km² (tons)

Key
food crops
cash crops
fruit and vegetables
cattle

1930 1957 1961 1977 1987

Learning to live sustainably in Machakos

People everywhere

NO HOMO SAPIENS (THAT'S US!)

200 000 years ago

170 MILLION OF US

Where are you?

Over here!

2000 years ago

900 MILLION OF US

Haven't I seen you before somewhere?

200 years ago

OVER 6,000 MILLION OF US. (6 BILLION)

HELP!

Today

How does the population rise so fast?

As you can see above, the number of humans on the Earth is rising fast. This shows what happened in one family …

Did you know?
◆ The Earth's population is growing by about 9000 people an hour.

1750

Bo and Ella fell in love. They got married and had **4** children.

1780

All 4 of these had children of their own. **18** altogether.

1820

16 of the 18 in turn had children of their own – **76** altogether.

So Bo and Ella's family just kept on growing,
It has been like this all over the world, for centuries.
So it's easy to see how the population has risen so fast.

Birth rate and death rate

Every year, millions of humans die. But the population still keeps rising!

NATURAL INCREASE = BIRTH RATE – DEATH RATE

We won.

Just you wait!

1000 people live in country X. If 20 babies are born there this year, the **birth rate** is 20 births per 1000.

If 3 people die there this year, then the **death rate** is 3 deaths per 1000.

17 more births than deaths – so the **natural increase** in the population this year is 17 per thousand or 1.7%.

Your turn

1 What does *population* mean?

2

How the human race has grown	
Year	Population (billions)
10 000 BC	0.004 (which is 4 million)
5000 BC	0.005 (or 5 million)
1000 BC	0.05 (or 50 million)
1 AD	0.2 (or 200 million)
1000	0.3 (or 300 million)
1600	0.5 (or 500 million)
1800	1.0 (or 1000 million)
2000	6.0 (or 6000 million)

A graph for this table is started below.

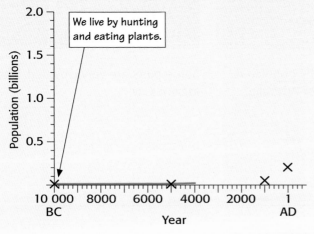

We live by hunting and eating plants.

a Each tiny division on the lower axis represents:
  i 50 years? ii 100 years? iii 200 years?
b Make a *large* copy of the axes started above.
  Continue the lower axis to **2400 AD**.
  Continue the side axis up to **8 billion**.
  (Use a full page, or even two joined together.)
c Plot the eight points from the table, and add a title.

3 Now add these notes to your graph. The first one has been written on the graph above, as an example.

At this year ...	write this ...
10 000 BC	We live by hunting and eating plants.
9000 BC	The first farms appear.
7500 BC	The first towns appear.
4500 BC	The wheel is invented.
3000 BC	The first cities appear, and the first writing.
1000 BC	The Iron Age starts. (We begin using iron for tools and weapons.)
43 AD	The Romans invade Britain.
400 AD	The Romans leave Britain.
1750 AD	The Industrial Revolution starts. (We begin using engines and build lots of factories.)

4 Look at your graph.
  a Write a sentence to describe its shape.
  b If the Earth's population keeps growing like this, about what will it be in the year 2200?

5 These helped the Earth's population to grow faster. See if you can explain why.

A the discovery of iron

B the Industrial Revolution

6

The island of Timu, 1995	
Population at the start of the year	2000
Number of births during the year	60
Number of deaths during the year	40

Using the data in this table, work out:
a the birth rate for Timu that year
b the death rate for Timu that year
c its population at 31 December 1995
d the natural increase that year (as a %).

7 Look at these two lists:

1 Changes in a country
a Everyone gets better food to eat.
b A terrible war breaks out.
c A deadly disease spreads.
d There is a severe famine.
e More hospitals and doctors are provided.
f Birth control pills are provided.
g More and more women get good jobs.

2 Possible results
A Death rate rises.
B Death rate falls.
C Birth rate rises.
D Birth rate falls.
E No effect on birth or death rates.

For each change in list **1** choose the likely result(s) from list **2**. (You can choose more than one result.)
Write your answer like this: d → A + ___ .

So where is everyone?

People are not spread evenly around the world.

Some places, like Antarctica, are empty. Far too cold to settle here!

Some parts are lightly populated. For example much of Australia.

Some parts are very crowded. Like Mexico City.

The world's population density

The map below shows how we are spread around the world.
There are many reasons why we are spread like this.
The map in **Your turn** will give you some clues.

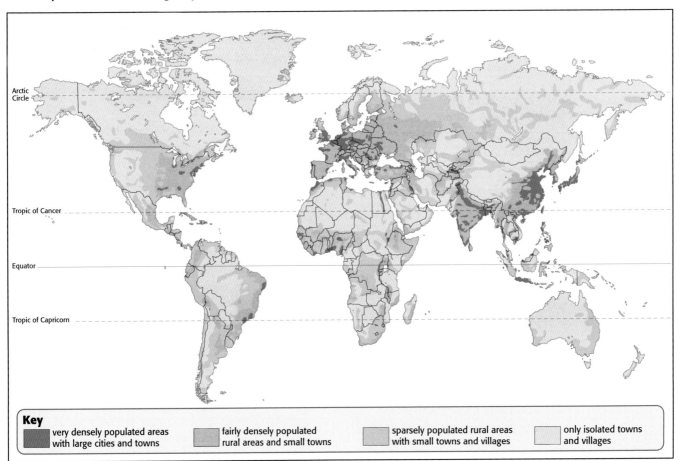

Arctic Circle

Tropic of Cancer

Equator

Tropic of Capricorn

Key

very densely populated areas with large cities and towns

fairly densely populated rural areas and small towns

sparsely populated rural areas with small towns and villages

only isolated towns and villages

Your turn

The world map on pages 124–125 will help with these.

1 Look at the key for the map on page 62.
   What does this term mean?
   a sparsely populated   b isolated
   (Try to answer without looking in the glossary.)

2 Name two countries that are:
   a very crowded, overall   b very lightly populated

3 In general, where do more people tend to live?
   a in the middle of continents
   b on or near the coast
   See if you can come up with a reason for this.

4 Climate affects all living things. It is one reason why
   some regions are less crowded than others.
   a What's the climate like at A on the map below?
   b This shows what crops need:

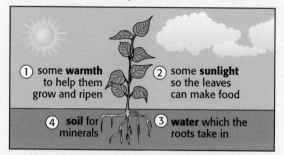

① some **warmth** to help them grow and ripen
② some **sunlight** so the leaves can make food
④ **soil** for minerals
③ **water** which the roots take in

   Will crops grow well at A? Give reasons.
   c Is the population density at A high, or low?
   Give as many reasons as you can to explain why.

5

Place	Country	Climate	Population density	Reasons
B				

Make a table like the one started above, but much larger.
Leave room to write quite a lot in the last column.

a Write the letters B, C, D and E from the map below,
   in the first column.
b Name the countries they're in, in the second.
c Describe the climate at each place in the third column.
   (Use the key, and what you know already.)
d In the fourth column describe the population density
   at each place, using one of these phrases:
   very high   fairly high   fairly low   very low
e In the last column give as many reasons as you can
   to explain why the population density is like this.

Key

Hot tropical rainy climates
- rain all year
- monsoon
- dry in winter

Very dry climates
- no reliable rain
- a little rain

Cold polar climates
- no warm season and fairly dry

Warm summers, mild winters
- dry in summer (Mediterranean climate)
- dry in winter
- no dry season

Cool climates
- rain all year
- dry in winter

Mountain climates
- the higher you go, the colder it gets

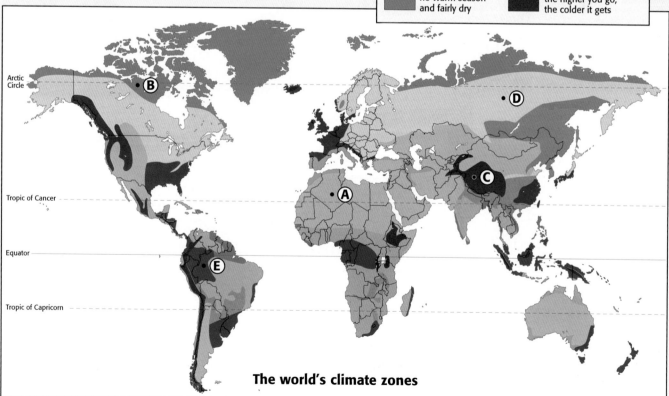

The world's climate zones

Resources are all the things we need to live and work.
Look at the resources this person needs. (Guess who?)

1 He needs food – a lot of it. Just ten minutes ago he got through a whole loaf …

… which was made from wheat. And wheat needs soil and rain.

2 He needs water. Some to drink, and lots for his long hours in the bathroom …

… which means he needs rain, and rivers. And pumps and pipes to bring the water to him.

3 He needs air. He breathes in about 17 000 times a day, and takes in about 0.5 litres of air each time.

socks from his granny

4 He needs warmth. He just hates cold rooms …

… and that means he needs fuel. In his house they burn North Sea gas as fuel for heating and cooking.

5 He needs clothing. His granny insists on knitting his socks – 5 pairs of black socks every birthday.

They're made of wool. So they need sheep … which need grass, and soil, and rain …

6 He needs textbooks for school work, and novels to read …

… and they need paper, which is made from trees …

… and metal saws to cut down the trees, and metal machines to print and cut the pages.

7 He needs money of course. For computer games, CDs, magazines, and the cinema.

So Walter needs quite a lot of resources to keep him going. And so do you!

You use some resources directly. For example water. You use others indirectly. For example the soil your lunch grew on, and the trees and printing machine used to make this book.

Putting resources into groups

We can put resources into groups. Like these:

◆ natural or primary resources.
   They come from the Earth or the atmosphere.
   Example: water, crops.
◆ manufactured resources.
   Made by people, often from natural resources.
   Example: a printing machine.
◆ basic resources.
   We would die without these.
   Example: air.
◆ renewable resources.
   We can recycle them non-stop, or grow more.
   Example: water, crops.
◆ non-renewable resources.
   Once we use them we can't make or grow more.
   So we will run out of them one day.
   Example: metals, North Sea gas.

A resource can belong to more than one group.

All this for socks?

Your turn

1 Look at all the resources Walter needs.
   a What is a resource?
   b Some of them, like air, are natural resources.
     What does that mean? Give two more examples.
   c Some are non-renewable. What does that mean?
   d Is sheep's wool a renewable resource?
   e Are sheep a renewable resource?

2 a Now make a large copy of the table below.
     You may want to turn your page on its side.
   b In the second column, write what Walter needs
     the resource for. One has been filled in for you.
   c Now put ticks in the correct places in the other
     columns. For example air is a basic resource,
     natural, free and renewable – so four ticks.

The resources Walter needs	He needs this for	Basic	Could survive without it	Natural	Manufactured	Free	Not free	Renewable	Non-renewable
A resource he uses directly									
air	breathing	✔		✔		✔		✔	
water									
food									
North Sea gas									
clothing									
money									
books									
A resource he uses indirectly									
soil									
grass									
trees									
metal									
water treatment works									

The trouble with resources

Meet Jintana who lives in Thailand, 9000 km from Walter on the other side of the world. Just like Walter, she needs resources …

2 She needs water. For drinking, cooking and washing. But there are no water taps in her home …

1 She needs food. She's preparing a meal for the family right now – supervised by her little brother.

… so two hours from now she'll walk a kilometre to the public pump and carry two buckets of water home.

3 She needs air. Luckily, air is everywhere and it's free.

They don't have a lot to eat. But enough. They eat the same thing most days.

But it's not always healthy. The air in here gets full of smoke from the fire and fumes from the oil lamp. Bad for her lungs.

6 She'd like money, to go to school in the next town. So that she can study hard and get a good job one day …

5 She needs clothing. The clothes she's wearing once belonged to her cousin in the city.

4 She needs fuel to cook with …

… but no chance. With five children and a tiny farm her parents have no money to spare.

She has never had new clothes of her own – but she'd really love some.

… but there's no gas in her home. She burns wood from the trees her father chops down, in this open fire.

Jintana is not starving. She has food and shelter and a family she loves. But she does not have many of the resources Walter takes for granted. Resources are not shared equally between people, or countries. Just think about this:

- around 1.4 billion people can't get clean safe water
- around 3 billion people don't have toilets.

Did you know?
- Tonight about 100 million people will sleep outside – they have no homes or shelter.

For example … food

We all need food to help us grow, and for energy.
The energy from food is measured in **calories**.

We need 1600 calories a day just to lie in bed and do nothing.
And at least 2200 calories to get through a normal day.
But many people have to survive on less, as this map shows.

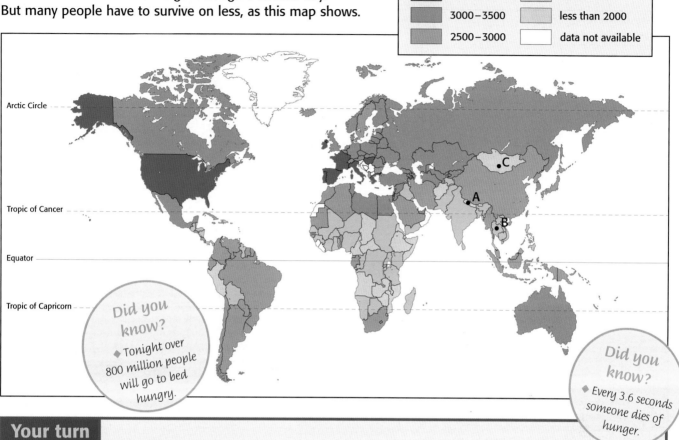

Key
Average daily food intake in calories per person

- over 3500
- 3000–3500
- 2500–3000
- 2000–2500
- less than 2000
- data not available

Did you know?
◆ Tonight over 800 million people will go to bed hungry.

Did you know?
◆ Every 3.6 seconds someone dies of hunger.

Your turn

1 Jintana lives at A, B or C on the map above. Which one? (The map on pages 124–125 will help.)

2 Jintana's home is quite different from Walter's. Make a table like this, and fill it for both of them. Use clues from pages 64 and 66 to help you.

	Jintana's home	Walter's home
Running water		
Flush toilet		
Electric light		
Gas cooker		
Fridge		
Washing machine		
Lots of cupboards		

3 Jintana and Walter have quite different lives too. Which of them do you think:

a does more physical work?

b is more likely to get a well-paid job?

c is more likely to take holidays?

d is more likely to be happy? Think carefully about this. Then explain your answer.

4 Jintana and Walter are lucky – both get enough to eat. Many people don't. Look at the map above.

a Name four countries where people have less than 2000 calories a day, on average.

b Do you think *everyone* in those countries has too little to eat? Explain.

5 a Now name four countries where people take in over 3500 calories a day, on average.

b Do you think this is a good thing?

6 Which *continent* is most short of calories?

7 'The more crowded a country is, the less calories people get.' Is this true or false?
Use the map on page 62 to help you decide.
Give three examples to support your answer.

8 Now, a challenge. Think of as many reasons as you can why people in some countries don't have enough food. You could show your answer as a big spider map. Here are some clues to help you.

drought   worn-out soil   fertilisers   money   imports education   food factories   roads   trucks

Fuel – just a store of energy

There's one resource we all need: **fuel**. A fuel is just a store of energy. We usually burn it to release the energy (as heat or light or movement). The energy in nearly every fuel comes from the sun …

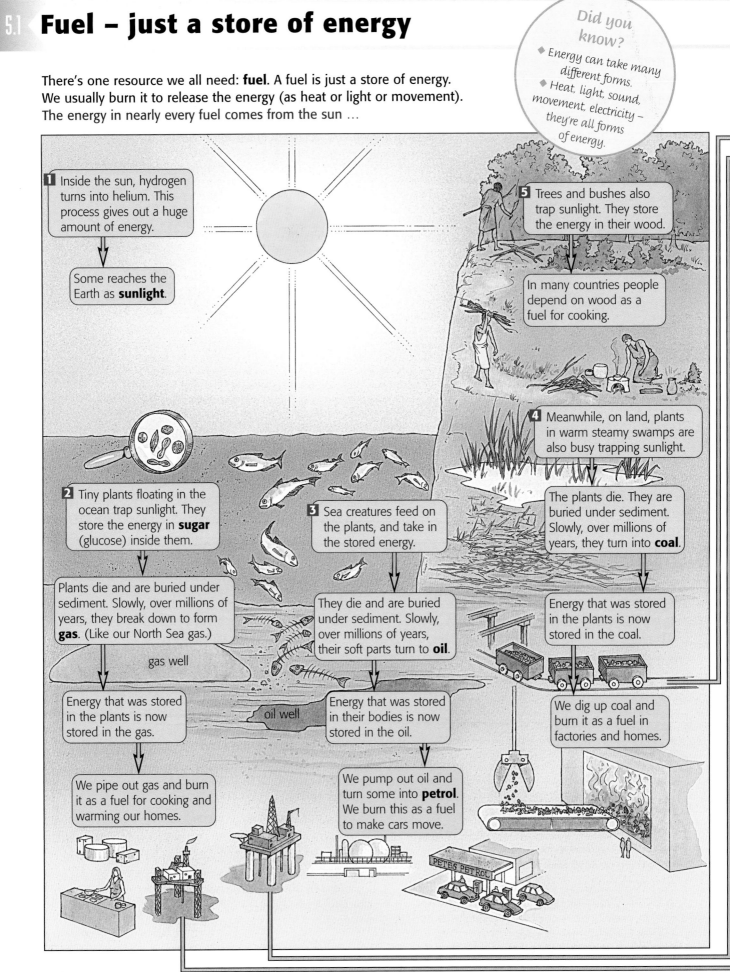

1 Inside the sun, hydrogen turns into helium. This process gives out a huge amount of energy.

Some reaches the Earth as **sunlight**.

5 Trees and bushes also trap sunlight. They store the energy in their wood.

In many countries people depend on wood as a fuel for cooking.

4 Meanwhile, on land, plants in warm steamy swamps are also busy trapping sunlight.

2 Tiny plants floating in the ocean trap sunlight. They store the energy in **sugar** (glucose) inside them.

3 Sea creatures feed on the plants, and take in the stored energy.

The plants die. They are buried under sediment. Slowly, over millions of years, they turn into **coal**.

Plants die and are buried under sediment. Slowly, over millions of years, they break down to form **gas**. (Like our North Sea gas.)

gas well

They die and are buried under sediment. Slowly, over millions of years, their soft parts turn to **oil**.

Energy that was stored in the plants is now stored in the coal.

Energy that was stored in the plants is now stored in the gas.

oil well

Energy that was stored in their bodies is now stored in the oil.

We dig up coal and burn it as a fuel in factories and homes.

We pipe out gas and burn it as a fuel for cooking and warming our homes.

We pump out oil and turn some into **petrol**. We burn this as a fuel to make cars move.

PETE'S PETROL

6 We also burn oil, coal, gas and even wood in **power stations** to give electricity – another form of energy!

7 Meanwhile, some minerals in the Earth contain unstable atoms. These break up over time, giving out lots of energy.

So we also dig these minerals up for fuel. We call them **nuclear fuel** and use them in **nuclear power stations** to give electricity. (Note that they give out energy without being burned.)

8 Electricity is carried around the country by cables. We use it for lots of things – TV, lights, boiling the kettle …

Running out of fuel?

Somewhere on the Earth, coal, oil and gas are still forming. But we are using them up millions of times faster than they can form. So we will run out of them one day. That's why we say they are **non-renewable**.

It's the same with nuclear fuels. The Earth contains only a certain amount of them. Once we have dug them all up – that's it, folks!

When will we run out ? This is what some experts think:	
At our present rate of use we could run out of …	in about …
oil	40 years
gas	60 years
coal	250 years

Your turn

1 A fuel is a store of energy.
  a Name five fuels.
  b What do we usually have to do to a fuel, to release its energy?
  c Name two forms the released energy takes, when you burn gas in a gas cooker.

2 When you travel to school by bus or car, you really travel by the sun's energy. Draw a strip cartoon to explain why. You could start like this …

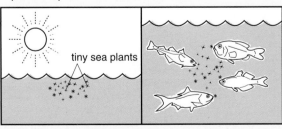

tiny sea plants

3 The energy stored in fuels can be changed into electricity. Give six examples of how electricity is used in your home.

4 Now make a larger copy of this table. In each box write a ✓ for yes, or a ✗ for no. One has been ticked for you. (You may need to use the glossary.)

Some different fuels				
	Stores energy from the sun	A fossil fuel	Used to generate electricity	A renewable resource
Gas	✓			
Oil				
Coal				
Wood				
Nuclear fuel				

5 Which of the fuels in the table might be used by:
  a Walter (page 64)?
  b Jintana (page 66)?
  Give reasons for your answers.

Bringing you electricity

You use electricity every day. So how is it made?

In 1831, Michael Faraday made an amazing discovery: move a magnet inside a coil of wire, and you get an electric current! And that's what we still do today.

In the power station they make or **generate** electricity by spinning a big magnet called an **electromagnet** inside a wire coil. They use **steam** to spin it, and a **fuel** to make the steam.

▲ *The electric Mr Faraday.*

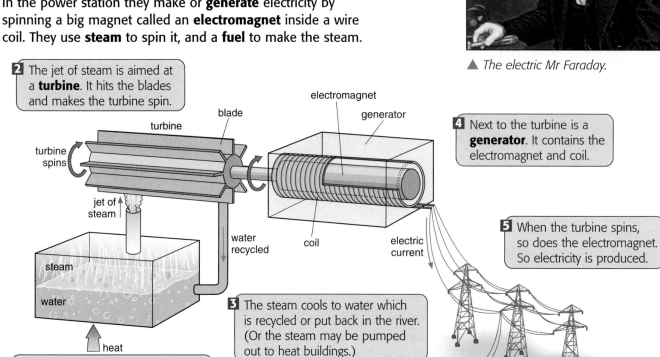

2 The jet of steam is aimed at a **turbine**. It hits the blades and makes the turbine spin.

turbine

turbine spins

blade

jet of steam

steam

water

heat

electromagnet

generator

coil

water recycled

electric current

4 Next to the turbine is a **generator**. It contains the electromagnet and coil.

5 When the turbine spins, so does the electromagnet. So electricity is produced.

3 The steam cools to water which is recycled or put back in the river. (Or the steam may be pumped out to heat buildings.)

1 First they boil water to make steam. They heat the water:
- by burning coal, oil, gas, wood or even rubbish as a fuel
- or using the heat given out by nuclear fuel.

6 Cables carry it away to homes, schools, offices and factories.

It doesn't have to be steam!

Steam is not the only way to spin a turbine ...

dam built on a river

turbines are set in the walls

turbine

2 This makes the air move and spin the turbine.

air

turbine

1 The waves move up and down in the sea.

In a **hydroelectric** station, fast-flowing **water** spins the turbines.

On a **windfarm** the wind spins them. The more wind the better!

Waves and the **tide** can also be used to make a turbine spin.

So – fast rivers, wind, waves and the tide can all give electricity.

From power station to you

Look at this map. It shows where electricity is generated in Great Britain.

The electricity is fed into a network of cables called the **National Grid**, and carried to your home, and all around the UK.

We use more electricity at certain times of day. For example more at breakfast time than at 4 am, when most people are sleeping. But it can't be stored. So each day:

◆ The National Grid company has to estimate how much electricity we will use for each half-hour of the *next* day.

◆ Then it plans with the power stations how much to generate each half-hour.

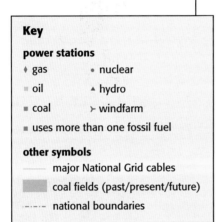

Key

power stations

◆ gas   • nuclear

▪ oil   ▲ hydro

▪ coal   ⊁ windfarm

▪ uses more than one fossil fuel

other symbols

—— major National Grid cables

▨ coal fields (past/present/future)

–·–·– national boundaries

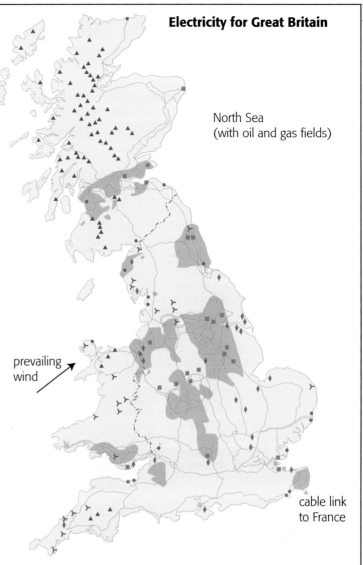

Electricity for Great Britain

North Sea
(with oil and gas fields)

prevailing wind

cable link to France

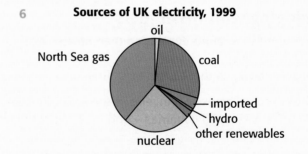

Your turn

1 Draw a flow chart to show how electricity is generated in a power station, using gas as a fuel.

2 Most power stations are at the coast or beside rivers. Why do you think this is?

3 a List *all* the energy sources from page 70 that can be used to generate electricity.
   b Now underline the ones that are *renewable*.

4 Look at the map above. (And at page 121.)
   a Where are most of the coal-burning power stations? Suggest a reason.
   b Where are most windfarms? Why?
   c Where are most hydroelectric stations? Why?
   d Nuclear power stations are usually built in remote areas, away from towns. Give a reason.

5 Explain why power stations generate more electricity:
   a in winter than in summer
   b when there's a big match on

6 **Sources of UK electricity, 1999**

oil

North Sea gas   coal

imported
hydro
other renewables

nuclear

Look at this pie chart for 1999.
About how much of our electricity came from:
a nuclear fuel?   b oil?   c coal?
d fossil fuels?   e hydro and other renewables?
Choose your answers from this list:
*two thirds   just under a quarter   one thirtieth
a bit less than one third   one sixtieth*

7 The UK *imports* some electricity. Suggest a reason for this. Say where we import it from, and how.

Why are the fossil fuels so important?

The fossil fuels – coal, oil and gas – are the world's main fuels, as this pie chart shows. Oil is number one.
And here are some reasons why they are so important …

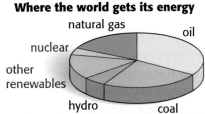

Where the world gets its energy

natural gas
oil
nuclear
other renewables
hydro
coal

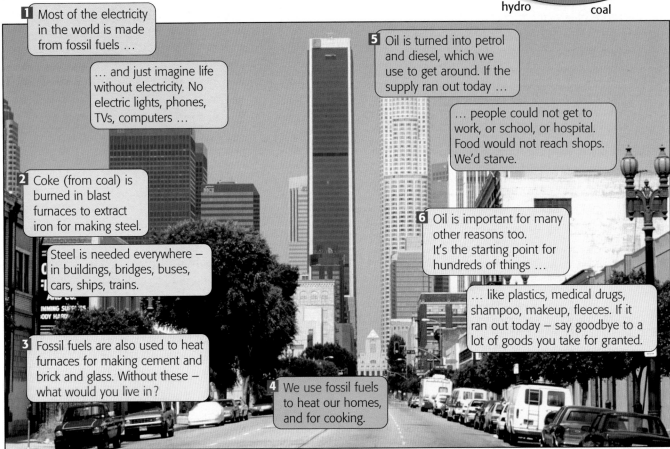

1 Most of the electricity in the world is made from fossil fuels …

… and just imagine life without electricity. No electric lights, phones, TVs, computers …

2 Coke (from coal) is burned in blast furnaces to extract iron for making steel.

Steel is needed everywhere – in buildings, bridges, buses, cars, ships, trains.

3 Fossil fuels are also used to heat furnaces for making cement and brick and glass. Without these – what would you live in?

4 We use fossil fuels to heat our homes, and for cooking.

5 Oil is turned into petrol and diesel, which we use to get around. If the supply ran out today …

… people could not get to work, or school, or hospital. Food would not reach shops. We'd starve.

6 Oil is important for many other reasons too. It's the starting point for hundreds of things …

… like plastics, medical drugs, shampoo, makeup, fleeces. If it ran out today – say goodbye to a lot of goods you take for granted.

Developing with fossil fuels

Some countries are more **developed** than others. That means they have better schools, hospitals, houses, roads, bridges, phone sytems and so on. As you saw above, all these need fossil fuels.

The photo above shows Los Angeles in the USA. The USA is one of the world's most developed countries – and it uses most fossil fuels.

So who has fossil fuels?

Like most resources, fossil fuels are not shared equally around the world. The map on the next page shows which countries produce them.

Countries without enough (or any) fossil fuels have to buy or **import** them from other countries. Or else do without.

Many poor countries can't afford to import much fossil fuel. So people in their rural areas depend on **firewood** for fuel. They may have to walk miles every day to find it.

▲ *Bringing home the fuel.*

Producing fossil fuels

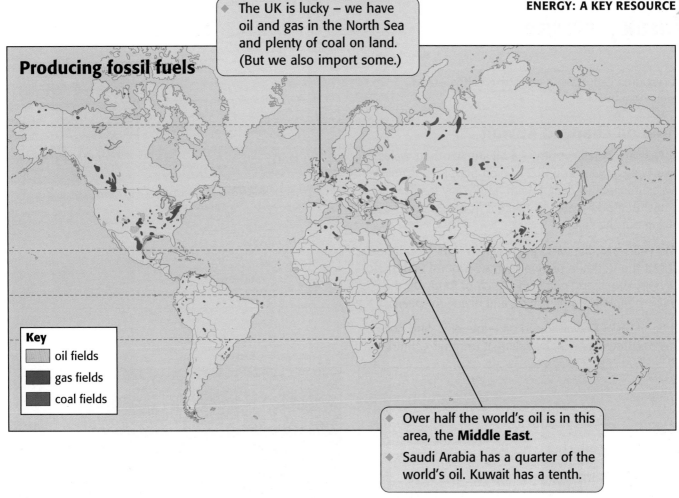

The UK is lucky – we have oil and gas in the North Sea and plenty of coal on land. (But we also import some.)

Key
- oil fields
- gas fields
- coal fields

- Over half the world's oil is in this area, the **Middle East**.
- Saudi Arabia has a quarter of the world's oil. Kuwait has a tenth.

Your turn

1 From morning to night, you depend on fossil fuels. Draw a spider map to show how. (You may need a full page.) You could start like this:

I depend on fossil fuels …

for these things I own …

my fleece

for these activities …

for these things I use …

watching TV   shampoo

2 The world gets most of its energy from fossil fuels. Some countries use a lot more energy than others. Dividing the total amount a country uses in a year by its population gives *the energy use per person*. Look at the table on the right.
  a Which of the countries has the highest energy use per person? Suggest reasons.
  b Which has the lowest? What does this tell you about that country?

3 Now draw a bar graph for the data in the table. Draw the bars horizontal, as on page 79. Turn your page sideways and use the full width.

4 Look at the photo at the bottom of page 72.
  a What does it show?
  b Why is this happening?
  c The women have to go a little further every day. Why? What could happen in the end?

5 Using the map on pages 124–125 to help you, name:
  a two European countries and two African countries that do not produce fossil fuels
  b four countries that produce all three fuels.

6 Page 68 shows that oil and gas form under the sea. But the map above shows they are found on land! How did they get there? Give an explanation.

Energy use per person (kilowatt hours a year)			
Australia	8000	India	350
Bangladesh	60	Kenya	120
China	650	UK	5100
France	5900	USA	11600

Lucky strike?

A resource can make a country wealthy – and cause war!

How oil changed Kuwait

Kuwait is a small country – a bit smaller than Wales. Like Wales it has around 2 million people. But unlike Wales it is mainly desert, with hardly any fresh water. It has to import water, or make it from sea water by taking out the salt.

100 years ago, life was very tough in Kuwait. Out in the desert the Bedouin people roamed around with their camels, sheep and goats, in search of food. On the coast, people lived by fishing and diving for pearls.

Then in 1938 Kuwait found oil – lots of it. And now it has become very rich, by selling it to other countries.

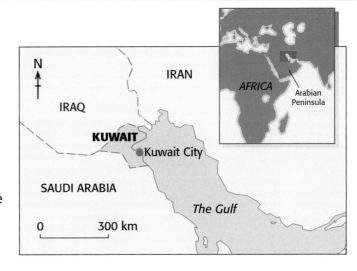

▲ *Kuwait City in 1938.*

▲ *And today.*

Kuwait at war

On 2 August 1990, the people of Kuwait woke up to a big shock: soldiers and army tanks everywhere! They had been invaded by Iraq.

All because of oil. Iraq felt that *it* really owned some of Kuwait's oil fields, along the border. And that Kuwait was selling too much oil, which meant Iraq could not sell so much.

Other countries (including the UK) took Kuwait's side. They sent soldiers, planes and ships to fight Iraq in the **Gulf War**. When it was over, Kuwait was free. But Kuwait and Iraq are still enemies.

▲ *The Gulf War, 16 January–28 February 1991.*

OPEC rules okay

When countries that sell oil gang up, they can hold everyone to ransom…

Did you know?
◆ A barrel of oil is 159 litres.

If there's a lot of oil to sell, the price falls. So the countries that sell it make less per barrel.

If there's not much to sell, the price rises – and the countries that sell it make more per barrel.

In 1960 officials from five oil countries met to talk this over. And they agreed to form …

… **OPEC**, the Organisation of Petroleum Exporting Countries. Today it has 11 members.

When OPEC cuts oil production, the price of oil rises everywhere. This affects everyone, even you!

Now many countries that import oil are trying to use less, and looking for other energy sources.

Your turn

1 Kuwait has changed a lot since 1938. Study the two photos on page 74 and describe the changes you can see.

2

Other changes in Kuwait	in 1960	in 1999
How long a new baby can expect to live	60 years	78 years
% of people aged 15 and over who can read and write a simple sentence	51%	79%

a This table shows that people in Kuwait are living longer now. Why do you think this is?

b Literacy has also improved.
  i What does literacy mean? (The table will help.)
  ii Give reasons why it has risen.

3 Kuwait could be in trouble when its oil runs out. Explain why.

4 When the price of oil rises it affects everyone. Draw a big spider map to show how. Like this:

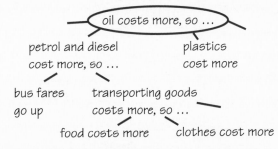

5 Which of these opinions do you agree more with? Give reasons.

5.5 The trouble with fossil fuels

Fossil fuels provide energy for our homes and cars and factories. Great! But they also do a whole lot of harm. Take oil as an example.

Did you know?

The UK pumps more than …
- 160 million tonnes of carbon dioxide
- 2 million tonnes of sulphur dioxide
- 2 million tonnes of nitrogen dioxide
- 300 000 tonnes of soot

into the air each year, by burning fossil fuels.

Oil and the environment

OIL REFINERY
PETES PETROL

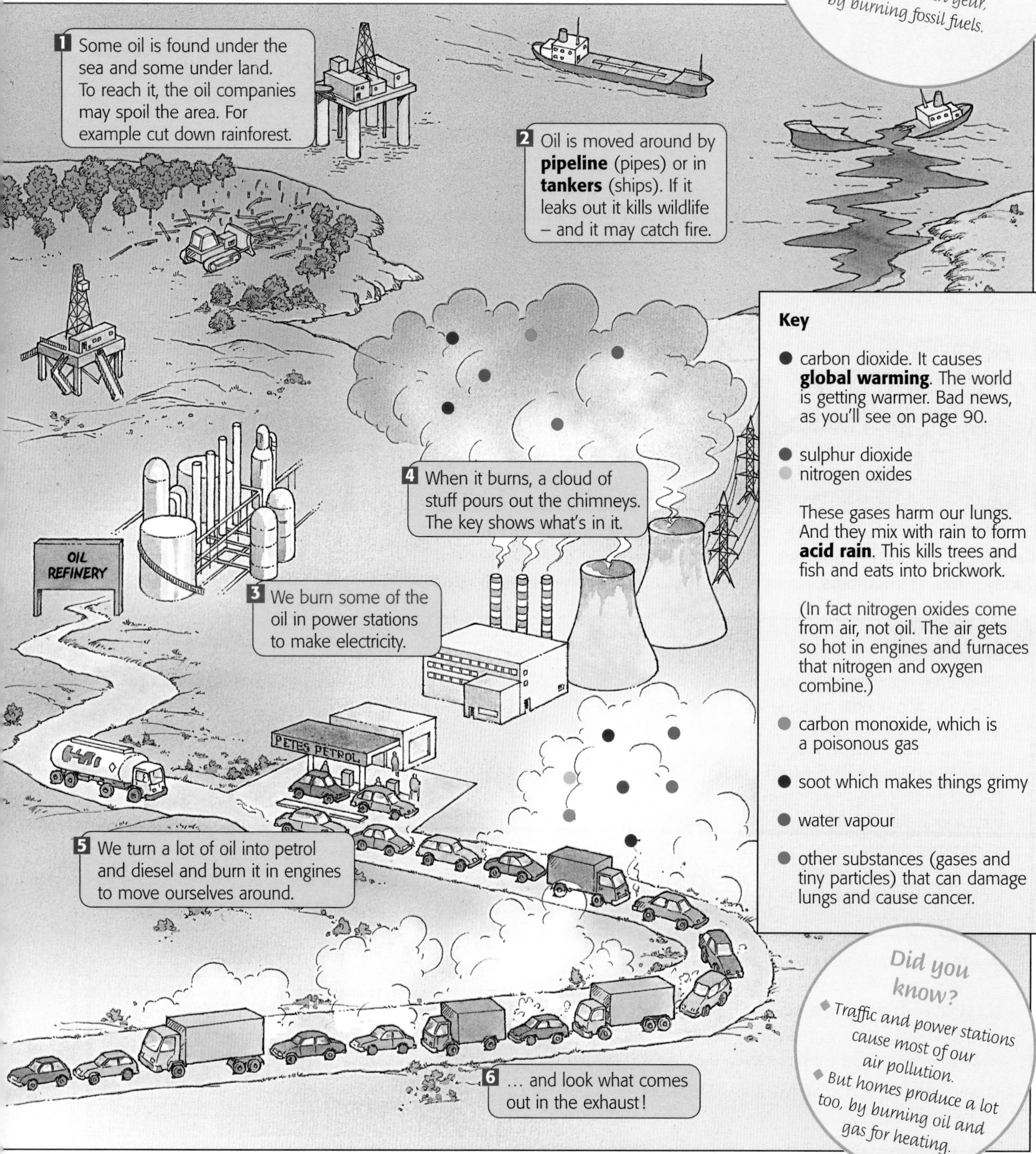

1 Some oil is found under the sea and some under land. To reach it, the oil companies may spoil the area. For example cut down rainforest.

2 Oil is moved around by **pipeline** (pipes) or in **tankers** (ships). If it leaks out it kills wildlife – and it may catch fire.

3 We burn some of the oil in power stations to make electricity.

4 When it burns, a cloud of stuff pours out the chimneys. The key shows what's in it.

5 We turn a lot of oil into petrol and diesel and burn it in engines to move ourselves around.

6 … and look what comes out in the exhaust!

Key

- carbon dioxide. It causes **global warming**. The world is getting warmer. Bad news, as you'll see on page 90.
- sulphur dioxide
- nitrogen oxides

These gases harm our lungs. And they mix with rain to form **acid rain**. This kills trees and fish and eats into brickwork.

(In fact nitrogen oxides come from air, not oil. The air gets so hot in engines and furnaces that nitrogen and oxygen combine.)

- carbon monoxide, which is a poisonous gas
- soot which makes things grimy
- water vapour
- other substances (gases and tiny particles) that can damage lungs and cause cancer.

Did you know?

- Traffic and power stations cause most of our air pollution.
- But homes produce a lot too, by burning oil and gas for heating.

What about the other fossil fuels?

All the fossil fuels:

- are taken from the Earth
- are transported to other places
- are burned to release energy.

Each step affects the environment – but the last step is the worst. Most of the world's air pollution comes from burning fossil fuels.

The table on the right compares what they give when they burn.

What the fossil fuels give out when they burn (kg of pollutant per billion BTU* of energy)			
Pollutant	Oil	Gas	Coal
Carbon dioxide	74 500	53 200	95 000
Nitrogen oxides	200	40	210
Sulphur dioxide	510	0.3	1180
Particulates (tiny particles of soot and other things)	38	3	1250

* BTU stands for British Thermal Unit

Did you know?
- *There are around 24 million cars on UK roads.*

Your turn

1 Draw a large spider map to show all the ways we damage the environment by using so much oil. You could start like this:

How we damage the environment over oil

finding it …

using it …

transporting it …

ocean floor disturbed

2 Look at the items you wrote on your spider map. Which of them affect:
   a just the place where the oil is found?
   Underline these in one colour.
   b other parts of the country?
   Underline these in a different colour.
   c other countries?
   Underline these in a third colour.
   Now write a colour key for your spider map.

3 Look at the table at the top of the page.
   a Do all three fuels add to global warming? Explain.
   b Which one may be worst for your health? Why?
   c Overall, which is worst for the environment?
   d Which one is 'cleanest'?

4 Photos A and B are linked to fossil fuels. For each:
   a describe what you see
   b say what you think caused it
   c say how long you think the effects will last (weeks? months? years?)

5 If we all saved energy we would use less fossil fuel. So we would help the environment.
   Write a list of steps *you* could take to save energy. (Like switch the light off when you don't need it?)

A

B

Global warming

Global warming means the Earth is warming up.
That might sound like a good thing – but it's a disaster.

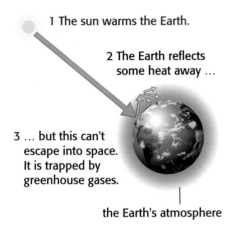

1 The sun warms the Earth.

2 The Earth reflects some heat away …

3 … but this can't escape into space. It is trapped by greenhouse gases.

the Earth's atmosphere

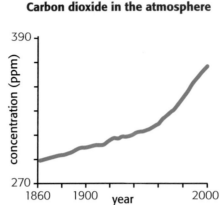

Carbon dioxide in the atmosphere

concentration (ppm) — 390, 270 — year 1860, 1900, 2000

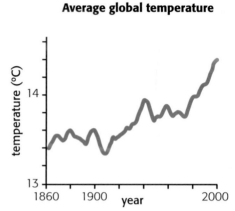

Average global temperature

temperature (°C) — 14, 13 — year 1860, 1900, 2000

All air contains a little carbon dioxide or CO_2. It is called a **greenhouse gas** because it traps in heat.

The amount of carbon dioxide in the atmosphere is rising, because of all the fossil fuel we're burning.

And the global temperature is rising to match, since more and more heat is being trapped.

Carbon dioxide is not the only greenhouse gas, but it's the main culprit.

How will global warming affect us?

This is what scientists predict …

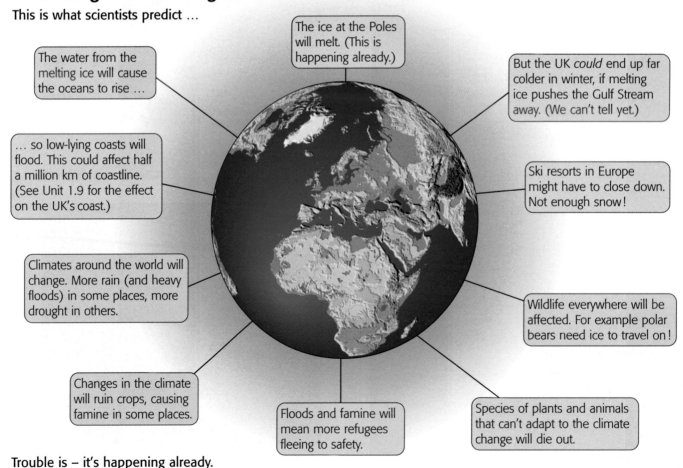

The ice at the Poles will melt. (This is happening already.)

The water from the melting ice will cause the oceans to rise …

But the UK *could* end up far colder in winter, if melting ice pushes the Gulf Stream away. (We can't tell yet.)

… so low-lying coasts will flood. This could affect half a million km of coastline. (See Unit 1.9 for the effect on the UK's coast.)

Ski resorts in Europe might have to close down. Not enough snow!

Climates around the world will change. More rain (and heavy floods) in some places, more drought in others.

Wildlife everywhere will be affected. For example polar bears need ice to travel on!

Changes in the climate will ruin crops, causing famine in some places.

Floods and famine will mean more refugees fleeing to safety.

Species of plants and animals that can't adapt to the climate change will die out.

Trouble is – it's happening already.

Spare a thought for the Arctic

Sitting in the daily traffic jam, you probably don't think about the Arctic. But soon you may have to.

A survey by scientists on the ship *The Arctic Sunrise* has shown that the Arctic ice floes are melting fast. They are up to a third thinner than 20 years ago. And an area the size of France has melted.

Melting ice means polar bears, seals and walruses can no longer find food for their young. The scientists found that the numbers of polar bear and seals have fallen – by as much as a half. The polar bear could be extinct in just 20 years.

But the problem does not stop there. Melting ice means rising sea levels. Many of the world's largest cities could drown in this century. And if the thaw continues the Atlantic Ocean will cool, changing the weather in places thousands of miles away.

Britain will be affected. Our mild climate is likely to become extreme, with more storms and floods. Sea levels could rise by up to a metre, drowning many coastal towns and villages.

The French, Dutch, Belgian and German coasts are in danger too. In the Mediterranean, holiday beaches could go under water. And warmer weather in the Alps could mean ski resorts close down.

The Arctic animals are telling us that global warming is already happening. It's real, it's here, it's now.

(From a newspaper article, 25 July 1999)

Did you know?
* With global warming, the UK could end up as cold as Moscow, in winter. (And that's freezing!)

▲ *What's happening to the ice?*

Your turn

1 Draw a diagram to show how carbon dioxide causes global warming.

2 Global warming will affect people everywhere. Draw a spider map to show all the ways it could affect us in the UK. You could start like this:

How global warming will affect the UK

low-lying coasts will flood

3 Some countries produce more carbon dioxide a year than others, because they burn more fossil fuel. Look at the bar graph on the right. It shows how much these countries produce *per person* in a year (the total amount divided by the population).

   a Which of them produces most carbon dioxide per person? Give reasons.
   (Think about the things it has lots of, like cars, dishwashers, factories …)

   b About how much carbon dioxide does the UK produce per person?

   c Which of the countries produces *least* carbon dioxide per person? Suggest reasons.

   d So will this country suffer *least* from global warming? Explain your answer.

4 Cars are responsible for much of the carbon dioxide we produce. How would you tackle this problem? Write a letter to the Minister for Transport giving your ideas.

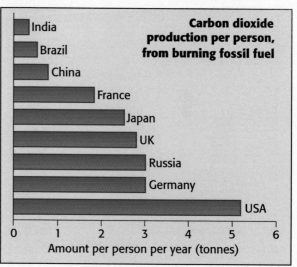

Carbon dioxide production per person, from burning fossil fuel

India
Brazil
China
France
Japan
UK
Russia
Germany
USA

Amount per person per year (tonnes)

Green electricity?

Our use of fossil fuels is not **sustainable**. They are harming the environment. *And* they'll run out one day.

Now everyone is worried about global warming. So the government wants us to get more electricity from **renewable** sources. Like this …

Wales's electric islands

All day long the tide rises and falls. Off parts of the Welsh coast the rise and fall can be huge – over 7 m. Now Wales plans to make use of this, by building two 'electric islands'.

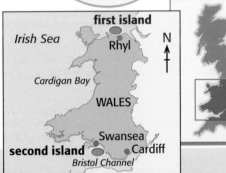

first island
Irish Sea
Rhyl
N

Cardigan Bay

WALES

Swansea
second island
Cardiff
Bristol Channel

1 This is the 'electric island' off Rhyl. It could produce 15% of the electricity Wales needs.

2 The hollow island covers an area of 50 square km. The walls are built of 30 million tonnes of rock.

3 It is really a round dam in three parts, with turbines set in the walls.

8 Boats and fish can just go round the island. And it's far enough from the coast not to spoil the view.

7 There are also plans for a fish farm inside, and a cycle path around the top!

6 There are plans for a windfarm on top of the island, to double the amount of electricity.

5 The island is in three parts so that water can be let out of each part separately, to meet the demand for electricity.

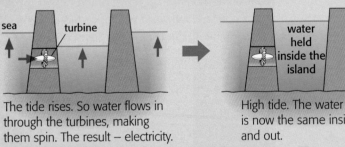
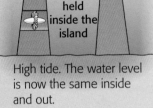

4 This is how each part works:

sea — turbine

The tide rises. So water flows in through the turbines, making them spin. The result – electricity.

water held inside the island

High tide. The water level is now the same inside and out.

The tide falls. Now the water is let out again. So the turbines spin the other way. More electricity!

Low tide. The water level is now the same inside and out, and the process is ready to start again.

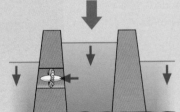

Electricity from willow trees

At Eggborough in North Yorkshire they are also making electricity in a sustainable way – from fast-growing willow trees.

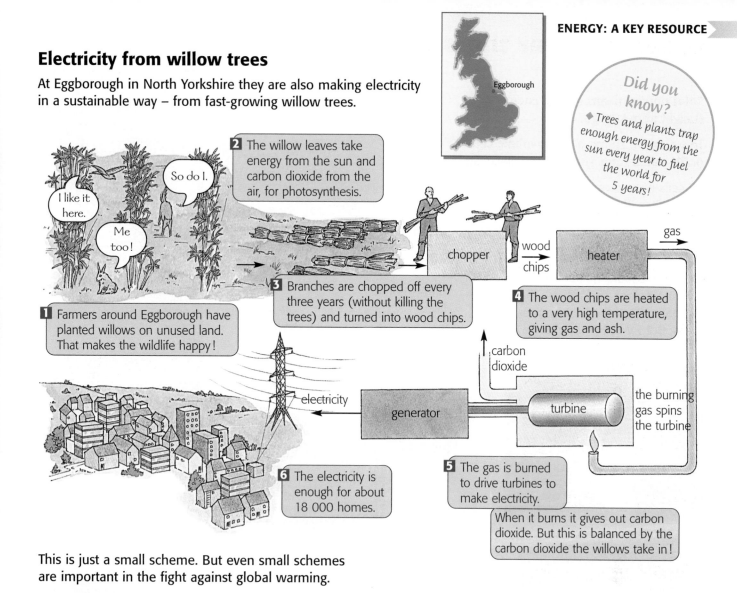

Did you know?
◆ Trees and plants trap enough energy from the sun every year to fuel the world for 5 years!

2 The willow leaves take energy from the sun and carbon dioxide from the air, for photosynthesis.

I like it here.

So do I.

Me too!

1 Farmers around Eggborough have planted willows on unused land. That makes the wildlife happy!

3 Branches are chopped off every three years (without killing the trees) and turned into wood chips.

chopper

wood chips

heater

gas

4 The wood chips are heated to a very high temperature, giving gas and ash.

carbon dioxide

electricity

generator

turbine

the burning gas spins the turbine

6 The electricity is enough for about 18 000 homes.

5 The gas is burned to drive turbines to make electricity.

When it burns it gives out carbon dioxide. But this is balanced by the carbon dioxide the willows take in!

This is just a small scheme. But even small schemes are important in the fight against global warming.

Your turn

1 What do you think 'green' electricity is? (Glossary?)

2 a Why does the tide rise and fall, and how often? (Page 7 will help.)

  b Wales is a good choice for the 'electric islands'. Why?

  c Give reasons why these islands are a good place to put wind turbines too. (One clue on page 71.)

3 Is the Welsh scheme *sustainable*? Explain. (Glossary?)

4
> To: BennyJones@rhylcouncil.net
> From: MaggieSwinburn@zillion.com
> ────────────────────────────────
> Mr Jones, my local school here in Wales has no money for books. They have one ancient computer. And now you plan to spend all this money on a crazy electric island with cycle paths. Get real!

You are Benny Jones, of Rhyl Council. Write a polite reply to Maggie telling her how the scheme will help Wales. (Decide whether an e-mail or letter is better.)

5 Now look at the willow scheme above.

  a Write down three good things about this scheme.

  b It produces carbon dioxide – but does not add to global warming. Explain why.

6 Copy this table. In each box put a ✔ for yes or ✗ for no. Add any more points you can think of.

Comparing the two electricity schemes	Tidal	Willow
Depends on the sun		
Depends on the moon		
Gives out carbon dioxide		
Uses a renewable resource		
Creates jobs for people	✓	
A good way to use waste land		
Could copy elsewhere in the UK		
Makes the environment look better		

Is solar power the answer?

Solar power means getting energy straight from sunlight.

This diagram shows a **photovoltaic cell** or **PV cell**. It turns sunlight into electricity!

PV cells were invented to make electricity in satellites. But now they're being used for other things.

A solar revolution?

Electricity usually needs expensive power stations, pylons and cables. That's why it still has not reached many poor rural areas. But PV cells may change all this.

when sunlight strikes the cell a current is produced

current collectors

silicon/boron layer

current

silicon/arsenic layer

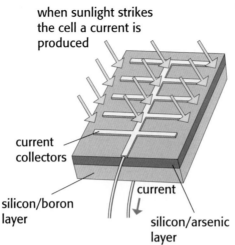

▲ Giant PV cells at an electricity company in the USA.

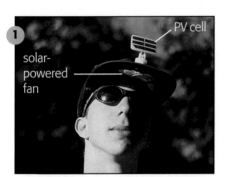

PV cell

solar-powered fan

▲ Walter, keeping cool in Liverpool.

▲ A street of solar-powered homes in Brazil.

▲ PV cells for sale in India.

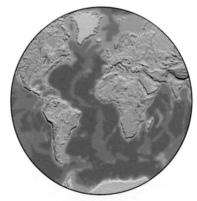

▲ Thrilled in Tibet with his solar-powered TV.

▲ A solar-powered fridge for vaccines saves lives in a clinic in Peru.

▲ Sewing goes solar in Ghana.

▲ A solar-powered ad in Egypt for you-know-what.

Sunshine supercar?

We already drive around on the sun's energy – stored in petrol. But now we can use it directly.

This shows a solar-powered car built by students in Arizona, USA. The PV cells are on the black 'lid'.

Even on a cloudy day in the UK there's enough sunlight to keep a car like this moving. Perhaps you'll have a solar-powered car one day.

Your turn

1 What is a photovoltaic cell? Describe in your own words what it does.

2 Look at the photos in this unit. Which use of solar power do you like best? Describe it.

3 Say whether these statements about solar power are true or false. (The photos will help.)
   A Every home could make its own electricity.
   B You must live near a city to use solar power.
   C Solar power is used only in rich places.
   D You could get a scooter to run on solar power.
   E It is not sunny enough in the UK for solar power.
   F Solar power is a renewable source of energy.
   G Solar power depends on fossil fuels.
   H Solar power makes global warming worse.

4 Look at the map below. What does it show?

5 a Which country gets the strongest sunshine, Greenland, Ireland or Saudi Arabia? Explain why. (Pages 124–125 will help.)
   b Which of them would be best for solar power?

6 Overall, which of the *continents* shown on the map would be best for solar power?

7 Using the map on page 73, name two *countries* with no fossil fuels, but very strong sunlight they could use for energy.

8 Now match each place in the photos on page 82 to the correct dot on the map. Start like this:
    =

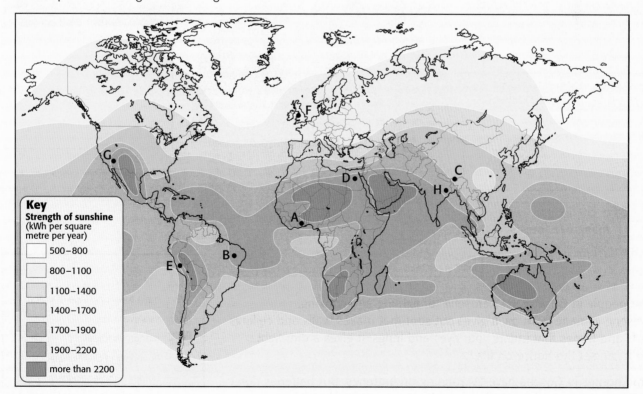

Key
Strength of sunshine
(kWh per square metre per year)
- 500–800
- 800–1100
- 1100–1400
- 1400–1700
- 1700–1900
- 1900–2200
- more than 2200

Going solar in Gosaba

Two billion people round the world have no electricity.
Most of them live in poor rural areas. Like the people of Gosaba …

This is Debu. He is 15. He lives in Gosaba, on a small island in an area called Sundarbans in India.

His home is the one on the right in this photo. It is made of wood, with a thatched roof. It has two rooms.

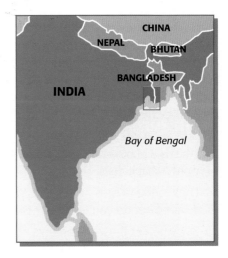

This sketch map shows Sundarbans and Debu's village.

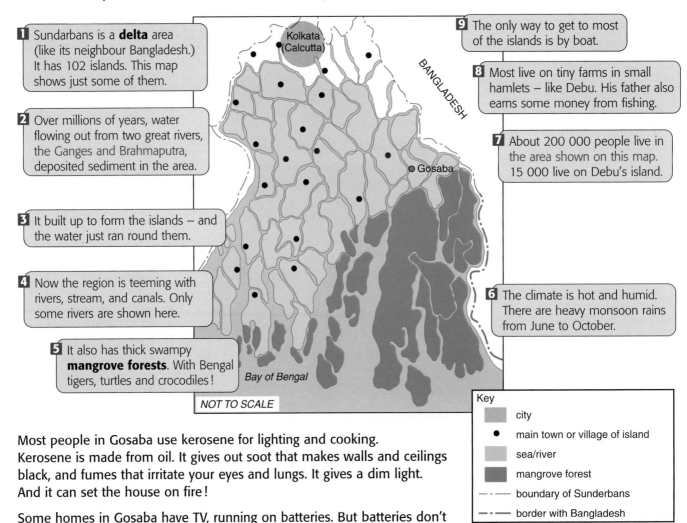

1 Sundarbans is a **delta** area (like its neighbour Bangladesh.) It has 102 islands. This map shows just some of them.

2 Over millions of years, water flowing out from two great rivers, the Ganges and Brahmaputra, deposited sediment in the area.

3 It built up to form the islands – and the water just ran round them.

4 Now the region is teeming with rivers, stream, and canals. Only some rivers are shown here.

5 It also has thick swampy **mangrove forests**. With Bengal tigers, turtles and crocodiles !

9 The only way to get to most of the islands is by boat.

8 Most live on tiny farms in small hamlets – like Debu. His father also earns some money from fishing.

7 About 200 000 people live in the area shown on this map. 15 000 live on Debu's island.

6 The climate is hot and humid. There are heavy monsoon rains from June to October.

Kolkata (Calcutta)

BANGLADESH

● Gosaba

Bay of Bengal

NOT TO SCALE

Key
- city
- ● main town or village of island
- sea/river
- mangrove forest
- --- boundary of Sunderbans
- ·—·— border with Bangladesh

Most people in Gosaba use kerosene for lighting and cooking. Kerosene is made from oil. It gives out soot that makes walls and ceilings black, and fumes that irritate your eyes and lungs. It gives a dim light. And it can set the house on fire !

Some homes in Gosaba have TV, running on batteries. But batteries don't last long, and cost a lot. Which means less money for other things.

Solar power arrives

In 1997, some homes and other buildings in Gosaba got solar power, as a trial. Debu's home was one.

The governments of India and the USA paid for most of the project. But the users also had to pay a little – £23 a year for 5 years.

Debu likes the two new lights in his house. Now he can play cricket after school and put off his study till later! Solar powered TV is good too. He does not get sent to the market any more for new TV batteries, or to get the old ones recharged.

▲ *Up go the PV cells on Debu's roof …*

◀ *… and on go the lights!*

Your turn

1 Debu lives on an island called Gosaba, in a region called Sundarbans.
   a In which country is Sundarbans?
   b In which continent is it?
   c Which country is it next to?

2 Give reasons why:
   a there are lots of islands in Sundarbans
   b the soil there is fertile
   c floods are a problem there.

3 India has a National Grid for electricity, like the UK. Give reasons why it hasn't reached Gosaba.

4 Before solar power, Debu's family had just two kerosene lamps like this one.
   They lit them every evening when it got dark, around 6. What problems can kerosene lamps cause?

5 a The table on the right shows the results of a survey on Gosaba. Which was the most common reason people gave, for liking solar power?
   b Why is this reason so important to them?

6 Display the results of the survey in any way you like. For example you could draw a pictogram or bar graph. Make it look interesting!

7 You are Debu. Write to your cousin Kali in Kolkata (Calcutta) telling her about solar power and how it has affected your family.

Impact of solar power on people in Gosaba	
Benefit	% who mentioned this
Better light	80
No fumes to irritate the eyes	85
Less coughing	10
Can earn more now since can work longer hours	25
Easier to serve food now	12
Easier to use than kerosene	64
Helps children to study	88
Can watch more TV news	44
Can watch more TV serials and films	78

A crime story

Sometimes a crime turns to tragedy. Like this one …

The offender's story

It happened a year ago when I was 13.

I was walking through the park with my friend and we were just talking about things we'd like to have. You know, clothes and all. There was a woman in front of us, quite old. My friend said 'I'm going to get her bag'. He ran and grabbed the bag. She held on and screamed 'Go away, go away'. He gave a tug. So did I. She fell back on to the iron railings.

Now she's paralysed. I am sorry about her. I got an 18-month sentence. It wasn't even my idea, but I didn't try to stop my friend so they said I was guilty too.

I wish it had never happened. But it did and I can't change it. Now I have a criminal record and the police will always be watching me.

At school they teach you things like cooking, and crossing the road safely, and what to do in a fire. But they never teach you not to steal – not really.

▲ *The offender.*

The victim's story

It has ruined my life. 46 years old, and in a wheelchair. I had a good job at the hotel. My children were doing well. We were just an ordinary family.

And then in just a few minutes everything changed. What did I do to deserve this?

The worst part is the effect on my family. It's like a big dark cloud over all of us, day in day out. We can never have a normal life again.

My husband had to leave a job he loved and take a part-time job to look after me. The children worry all the time about me. My son has got really depressed. He used to do well at school but now he's getting bad reports, and he'll probably fail his exams.

I never go out now – I sit out the back in the garden. When my husband wheeled me down the street, I got really panicky. I felt everyone was staring at me.

Those two boys just got a few years between them. I got a life sentence.

▲ *The victim.*

So – who pays the penalty?

In this sad story, the offenders were punished for their crime. The victim was punished too. But they were not the only ones who suffered, as you'll see next.

Paying for crime

90 km

Key

The victim and her family

The victim and her family live here.

This is the park where the crime took place.

The victim had to have several serious and expensive operations in this hospital.

The offenders and their families

The secure accommodation where the two boys are being held. They are not allowed out.

The families of the two boys live in these houses. Their neighbours won't talk to them now.

Other people

Five people in these houses need operations. But the hospital had to delay them in order to treat the victim. (It ran short of money.)

Eleven people in these houses used to walk in the park. Not any more. They are too afraid.

The owner of this house wanted to sell it last year – but the crime put buyers off.

The police and prisons cost a lot to run. The money comes from taxes …

… so everyone who pays taxes pays more because of crime.

Your turn

1 Why do you think the boy wanted the bag?

2 Who suffered because of this crime? Make a list.

3 The boy who snatched the bag was 11. He got an 18-month sentence too. Do you think it was fair that:
  a both boys got the same sentence?
  b they got 18 months?

4 Write down the meaning of each term. (Glossary?)
  victim   offender   sentence
  secure accommodation

5 We all pay for crimes other people commit. You pay every time you go shopping! Look at this:

Theft from UK shops costs £ billions every year!

To see how you pay for shop theft, write these sentences in the correct order.

A The shop has to find money to pay for the stolen goods and the security staff.

B So the shop hires security staff to stop theft.

C Shoplifters steal things from a shop.

D So you pay more when you go shopping.

E So it charges more for the things it sells.

6 Mugging and shoplifting are crimes. So is dumping poisonous chemicals in rivers. Which do you think is the best definition of crime?
  a An action that harms a person.
  b An action that breaks the law.
  c An action that offends people.

Different kinds of crime

It's a bad bad day in the city …

7 Two boys are spraying graffiti on the railway bridge.

1 In a back room, a man is selling new computers. Only £200 each. (His mate stole them from a truck last week.)

8 On the 2.30 train, nine people are travelling without a ticket.

14 In a secret room, three people are working very hard, printing fake £5 notes.

9 In a restaurant, they're serving meat that's gone off. They hope no-one will notice.

15 A woman drives herself home from lunch in a pub – even though she is tipsy.

2 Three cars on this street are parked on double yellow lines.

16 At this corner, one young man has just stabbed another to death, because of the colour of his skin.

10 The head office of a company. Fumes from its factories around the UK are damaging people's lungs.

3 In a shop a young woman is buying a coat using a stolen credit card.

17 A man has just parked a car outside the embassy. It contains a bomb that will go off in 15 minutes.

4 A husband has just beaten his wife up again. Her face is bruised and bleeding.

11 The owner is out. But a stranger is climbing in a window and will steal her jewellery.

18 Two men in balaclavas have just walked into a shop. One aims a gun at the staff while the other lifts cash from the tills.

5 A woman is busy writing lies on a tax form, so that she won't have to pay much tax.

12 A boy has just broken into a battered old car and is driving it away.

19 An older boy has just caught a 12-year-old in a headlock and snatched his mobile phone.

13 In the school three girls are bullying another girl. They slap her face and push her over.

6 Three people in here are watching TV. No TV licence.

20 In the corner shop, the shopkeeper is selling cigarettes to a girl of 13.

(But luckily, many good things happened in the city that day too.)

How much crime is there?

The UK has quite a lot of crime (but most of it is not very serious crime). The police record some of it – but not all crime is reported to them.

So every two years the government carries out a big crime survey. Households in England and Wales are asked about crimes such as burglary that they may have suffered over the past twelve months.

This survey shows up far more crimes than the police records do – in fact up to four times as many! The table on the right shows the results for one year. There were over ten million thefts.

But the survey does not ask about crimes such as fraud or drug dealing, for example. So you need to look at police records too, to get a clear picture.

Type of crime		Number of times committed (thousands)
1 Vandalism		2917
2 Thefts	burglary	1639
	of or from cars	3483
	of bicycles	549
	other household thefts	2067
	other thefts from people	2397
	Total	10 134
3 Violent crimes	mugging (to rob)	390
	wounding (in fights)	714
	common assault (hitting)	2276
	Total	3381
Total of all crimes		16 437

British Crime Survey: one year's results

Your turn

1 First, pick a number from the photo to match each term below. (A different number for each.)

a murder   b forgery
c vandalism   d armed robbery
e burglary   f domestic violence
g fraud   h handling stolen goods
i a traffic offence   j environmental crime
k terrorism   l common assault
m car theft   n mugging

If you get stuck the glossary *may* help.

2 Both young people and adults commit crime. Look at the list of crimes a–n above. Pick out:

a *one* you think is most likely to be carried out by young people (under 16)

b *five* more likely to be carried out by adults

c *two* you think just as likely for either group.

3 Young people are often victims of crime. From the photo, pick out *five* crimes where young people are, or could be, victims.

4 All the crimes on the photo took place in a city. But some of them could take place in a rural area. Give the numbers for *four* crimes:

a that could easily take place in a tiny rural hamlet

b unlikely to take place in a rural area.

5 Many crimes are not reported to the police. Suggest a reason why these crimes from the photo were not reported.

a **12**   b **4**   c **20**   d **13**

6 Look at the table above.

a How many crimes did the survey find altogether? (Check the heading of the last column!)

b Of the three main groups of crime, which was the most common?

c There were nearly three million acts of vandalism. Give four examples of vandalism.

d There were more thefts than violent crimes. About how many times more?

e Which type of theft was the most common? Give a reason.

f Which type of theft was the least common? Give reasons.

g Many thefts are from households. Name four things that might be stolen in household thefts.

7 All the crimes on the photo are wrong. But some are more serious than others.

a Draw a scale like this. Make it 12 cm long and divide it into three equal parts.

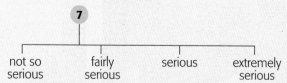

not so serious   fairly serious   serious   extremely serious

b Now mark in these six crimes where you think they should go on the scale:

1   **2**   **8**   **9**   **10**   **17**

One circle has been drawn in as an example.

Did you know?
- Murder is quite rare compared with other crimes.
- There are about 13 000 times more thefts than murders!

Criminal geography!

Criminals go where their targets are – the people they want to harm, or the things they want to steal. And they do not want to get caught. So they think a lot about geography!

The criminal's mental map

As you saw on the last page, different places offer different **opportunities** for crime. Like shops to steal from or houses to burgle.

We all have **mental maps** (in our mind) of areas we know well. Look at this mental map for a criminal.

The criminal will commit crimes in the areas he knows well, where they overlap with areas of opportunity.

Look at his three crime areas. Note that a criminal usually won't commit crime *too* close to home. Why not?

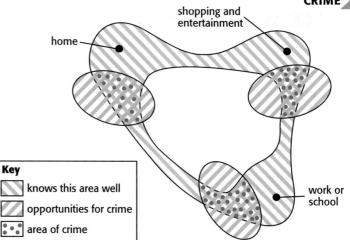

Key	
	knows this area well
	opportunities for crime
	area of crime

Your turn

1 Look at the places shown on the opposite page. Which would you feel least safe in? Why?

2 a What does the term 'criminal' mean? (Glossary.)

  b Explain why criminals might like the places in these photos:

    2   **3**   **4**   **5**   **6**

3 **Physical disorder** means messy, neglected, not looked after.

  a Pick out the photo that shows the highest physical disorder.

  b Write a paragraph to describe what you see.

  c What kind of crimes might you find here?

4 Look at the mental map above, for a criminal.

  a Make a larger copy of it.

  b On your copy mark in *three* likely crimes in each of the three areas of crime. Choose from this list:

    A shoplifting   B burglary
    C violent assault D selling drugs
    E vandalism   F picking pockets
    G car theft   H stealing money

    Write in just the letters (A, B, C …) on your map. You can use a letter more than once if you wish.

5 It's time to think about the victims.

  The table on the right shows the risk of burglary. 3.4 % of households in rural areas are likely to be burgled, and 5.6 % of all households.

  Draw a bar graph to show the data in the table. It will be a wide graph so you can turn your page sideways. Start like this:

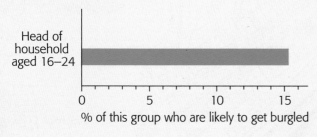

6 The clue box below gives *some* help for this question. Suggest reasons why the risk of being burgled is:

  a lowest in rural areas

  b low for people over 65

  c lower if you own your home than if you rent it

  d above average if you live on a main road

  e below average if you earn more than £30 000

  f higher for flats than for detached houses

  g highest where the head of the household is only 16–24.

CLUE BOX

Not everyone can afford burglar alarms and good locks.

Lots of us don't know our neighbours.

In busy places nobody pays much attention to strangers.

Burglars prefer places with no-one at home.

We take more care of our own things.

If you own lots of things you might fit a burglar alarm and good door and window locks.

The risk of household burglary	%
Head of household aged 16–24	15.2
Living in an area of high physical disorder	12.0
Living in rented property	9.7
Living in the inner city	8.5
Living in a council estate	8.1
Living in a flat	7.2
On a main road	6.6
Average risk of being burgled	5.6
Earning more than £30 000 a year	5.0
Living in property they own	4.2
Living in a detached house	4.1
Head of household 65 or older	3.8
Living in rural areas	3.4

Mapping crime

Criminals are interested in geography – and so are the police!
The police use maps and aerial photos to help them track crime.

It's time to put your police hat on. You are now in charge of crime control
for the area shown on the map below. The matching photo on page 93
will help you answer these questions. The ideas on page 88 will help too.

Your turn

1 There were several fights along one part of
   the High Street, in the last six months.
   a Suggest a reason for this. (Check building use!)
   b What could you do to prevent trouble here?
      Come up with some suggestions.
      Then put them in order, with the best one first.

2 Now look at square 1436.
   a What was the main crime here?
   b Suggest a reason for this. (Check the photo.)
   c What will you do to prevent this crime?
      Put your suggestions in order, best one first.

Key

railway and railway bridges

embankment

Businesses

shops (all types)

financial centres (banks,
building societies, post office)

places of entertainment (pubs,
clubs, wine bars, cafes, restaurants)

Abbreviations

PW place of worship
PO post office
Mkt market
Sta station

Crime over last 6 months

○ household burglary
○ repeat houshold burglary
○ break-ins to businesses
● assault (fighting)
● theft of or from cars
● illegal dumping of rubbish
● vandalism
● mugging

0   600 m

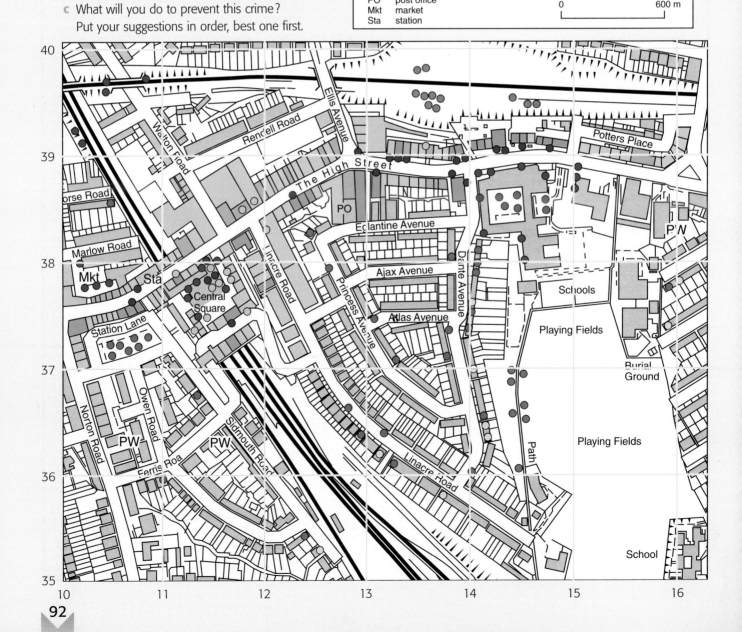

3 Yesterday two of your police team visited each house on the right of Dante Avenue (going north). They offered to write the postcode on valuable things like computers, with a special invisible ink.
   a What is a *postcode*?
   b Why did they want to write it on things?
   c Why did they choose this road?

4 Houses on the left of Dante Avenue are burgled far less often than those on the right. Suggest a reason.

5 Say which two grid squares were worst for this crime, and give reasons:
   a theft of or from cars
   b illegal dumping of rubbish

6 Vandalism is a problem too. Windows get broken, phone boxes smashed and walls sprayed with graffiti. It is a special problem in squares 1438 and 1137. Suggest reasons for this.

7 A **crime hotspot** has more crime than the other places around it. Where is the main crime hotspot in the map area? Try to give reasons for this.

8 Mr Williams rang yesterday to say he has now been burgled 6 times in 6 months. He lives at 126353. The photo below shows his house from the road.
   a There is one big reason why his house is burgled so often. What is it? (Use your eyes!)
   b Now write to Mr Williams with some advice about how he could stop his house being burgled.

The fight against crime

Criminals like an easy target – and not to get caught. And that gives us ideas about how to fight crime. Here are two methods …

1 Make the target harder to get at. This is called **target hardening**. You could put in high fences, window bars, and strong locks.

2 Make it easier to spot that a crime is being committed. You could fit burglar alarms and bright lights, and hire security guards.

Designing out crime

The **built environment** means all the built things around us – houses, streets, shopping centres and so on. As you have seen, it can give lots of opportunities for crime.

Now people are starting to think about crime *before* they build something new. They try to design it so as to prevent crime. This is called **designing out crime**. Look at this new housing estate:

Target hardening is built in.
◆ All windows have locks, and glass that's very hard to break.
◆ The outer doors are strong, with strong locks.
◆ Notice how every house has a burglar alarm.

The layout makes crime easier to spot.
◆ People can easily keep an eye on each other's homes and cars.
◆ There's only one way in and out of the estate. So burglars can't escape easily.
◆ All paths are out in the open, easy to see from the houses.

In this estate, the people have a **defensible space** around their homes. That means a space they can watch over easily and protect. Giving people a defensible space is a good way to fight crime.

Today, special police advisers will check the plans for new developments, to make sure they are anti-crime. They will even suggest which kinds of doors, windows and locks to use.

Your turn

1 What does 'target hardening' mean?

2 a First, make a larger copy of this Venn diagram.

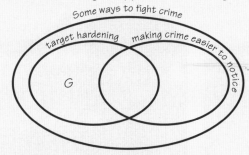

Some ways to fight crime

target hardening   making crime easier to notice

G

b Now look at the list below.
In which loop of your Venn diagram should each item go? Mark its letter in. (One is done already.)
If you think an item belongs to both loops, put the letter where they overlap.

A a lock for your bicycle
B a bullet-proof vest
C a 'krooklok' for a car steering wheel
D a CCTV camera (like the one shown on the right)
E security tags on clothes in a shop
F a guard dog
G a high wall with metal spikes on top
H a shatterproof glass screen in the post office
I a Neighbourhood Watch scheme (Glossary!)
J a bodyguard

3 CCTV (or closed circuit TV) is used in shops and on streets. Some years ago, CCTV cameras were installed in the town centre in Airdrie in Scotland. Look at this table.

Airdrie

	In the 12 months ...	
	before CCTV	after CCTV
Car break-ins	480	20
Theft of cars	185	13
Serious assaults	39	22
Vandalism	207	36
Break-ins to business premises	263	15

a Overall, did CCTV reduce the number of crimes?
b Which type of crime did it reduce most?
c Which did it reduce least? Try to give a reason.

4 You are (still) in charge of crime for the area on page 92.
You have money for just two CCTV cameras.
Below is a list of grid references.
From this list, pick out the two best places for your CCTV cameras, and give your reasons.
  a 145365   b 138375   c 113374
  d 139389   e 145385   f 115382

5 What do these terms mean?
  a designing out crime   b defensible space
Answer in your own words, using the photo at the bottom of page 94 to help you.

6 The methods in this unit help to reduce crime. But they don't stop it altogether! Look at these opinions:

If you want to cut crime, give young people interesting things to do.

To really cut crime we must teach people that it's wrong.

To get rid of crime – just get rid of poverty.

I think the best way to cut crime is to punish criminals very severely.

a Choose any *two* of the four opinions.
b For each, decide whether you agree or not. Then write down what you will say to that person in reply.

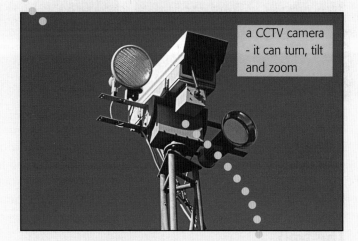

a CCTV camera - it can turn, tilt and zoom

The heroin trail

By the year 2000, most of the world's heroin came from Afghanistan. It was the country's biggest business.

It's 1999. This is Hamid, a poor farmer in Afghanistan. He needs money for his family. He can earn most by growing opium poppies …

… so he goes to the local drug trader, who gives him the seeds, and enough money to last him for several months.

He plants the poppy seeds in October on land where he used to grow wheat. By May 2000 the poppy is ready to harvest.

He takes a white liquid from the seed heads. This is opium gum. He sells it to the trader for about £30 a kilo. The gum …

… is turned into morphine. This is then turned into heroin. It is smuggled across the border to Iran, past the border patrols.

Two weeks later, in London, it is being sold for £20 000 a kilo. Emma is just about to spend £100 on it. In time it will ruin her life.

The trail

This map shows one route used to get heroin from Afghanistan to the British Isles.

♦ The heroin went through Iran. It entered Iran by truck, bike and camel.
♦ Big drugs traders sent 10 or 12 trucks at a time, loaded with several tonnes of heroin.
♦ This was worth millions of pounds so it had men with machine guns to protect it.
♦ From Iran most of the heroin went through Turkey. It was smuggled into the UK in trucks, ships, boats and planes.

As the heroin was moved, a lot got sold on the way. That's why Iran has many heroin addicts.

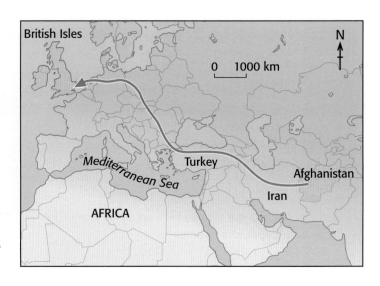

It's big business!

- The heroin trade is big business – worth billions of pounds a year.
- It ruins many millions of lives.
- It is an example of **organized crime**. It takes many people and a lot of planning to move heroin round the world.
- Many addicts commit theft and other crimes to get money for heroin – so they get into an even worse mess.

The fight against heroin

- Many countries have signed a **treaty** (agreement) to fight drugs.
- Even Afghanistan signed – but took very little action.
- So Iran spent millions putting up barriers and fences along its border with Afghanistan, to stop drug traffic.
- It put 30 000 soldiers on patrol along the border. Dangerous work! By the end of 1999 over 2000 Iranian soldiers had been killed by drug smugglers and over 10 000 wounded.
- In spite of all this, the heroin smuggling still continues.

▲ *Iranian soldiers scan the border.*

Your turn

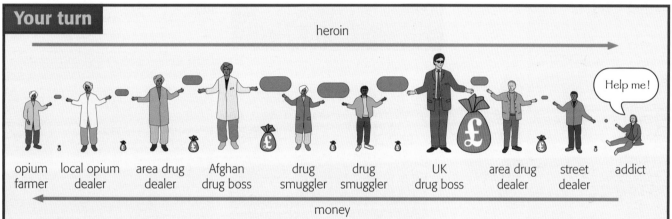

heroin

opium farmer · local opium dealer · area drug dealer · Afghan drug boss · drug smuggler · drug smuggler · UK drug boss · area drug dealer · street dealer · addict

Help me!

money

1 In which continent is Afghanistan?

2 In Afghanistan in 2000 there was a shortage of wheat in some places, for making bread. Suggest a reason.

3 The map on page 96 shows an overland drug route. List the countries the heroin passed through on this route, to get to the UK. (Pages 124–125 will help.)

4 a About how long is the border between Iran and Afghanistan?

　　150 km　　　　950 km　　　　1800 km

　b It is hard to patrol. Why? (Some clues in photos.)

5 Other countries have helped Iran to fight drug trafficking. (The UK gave bullet-proof vests for the soldiers.)

　a What is *drug trafficking*? (Glossary.)

　b Why did other countries want to help Iran?

6 Many drug traffickers tried to avoid the Afghanistan / Iran border. They got to Iran through other countries. Which country do you think a trafficker would choose, to get to Iran from:

　a southern Afghanistan?　b northern Afghanistan?

7 Drug trafficking is an example of *organized crime*. Explain the term in italics. (Glossary?)

8 Above is a chain of people involved in the drug business in the year 2000.

　a Most of the people in the chain got involved for one main reason. What was it?

　b Is each person in the chain a criminal? Explain your answer.

　c Why did the user start taking heroin? Suggest some possible reasons.

9 You're a world leader. You want to persuade Afghanistan (a poor country) never to grow opium poppies again. What will you do? Write an action plan.

10 Look at this opinion. Do you agree that drug dealing has no victims? Write down what you will say in reply.

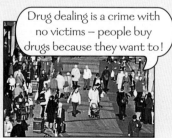

Drug dealing is a crime with no victims – people buy drugs because they want to!

Bem-vindos ao Brasil!

Welcome to Brazil! The fifth largest country in the world, with the fifth largest population. Where you'll find …

▲ … great food …

▲ … the world's largest rainforest, full of exotic plants and animals …

▲ … huge cities …

▲ … glorious sandy beaches …

60°

Equator

Tropic of Capricorn

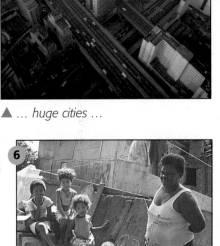

▲ … great poverty …

▲ … great wealth …

▲ … people of every race and colour …

▲ … spectacular scenery …

98

9

▲ … *a wealth of natural resources like diamonds, oil, iron ore …*

Some Portuguese to help you on your way

Hi!	Oi!
How are you?	Como vai?
Yes	Sim
No	Não
Please	Por favor
Thanks	Obrigado **(said by a male)**
	Obrigada **(said by a female)**
I love football.	Adoro futebol.
Geography is cool.	Geografia é legal.
See you soon.	Até logo.

10

▲ … *the world's best carnivals …*

11

▲ … *and football as king.*

Your turn

1 a In which continent is Brazil? (Page 124 will help.)
b Name all the countries in this continent that share a border with Brazil.
c Now name the two that don't.

2 Copy each statement and say whether it's true or false.
a Brazil covers almost half of South America.
b The equator runs through Brazil.
c Most of Brazil lies in the tropics. (Glossary?)
d Brazil lies beside the Atlantic Ocean.

3 Each photo shows a different image of Brazil. People say Brazil is a land of contrasts (opposites). Pick out any two images that you think show a big contrast, and describe them.

4 Of the eleven images of Brazil in this unit, which would you choose:
a for a tourist brochure? (No more than four.)
b for an article in a geography magazine about Brazil's natural features?
c for an article about *inequality* in society? (Glossary.)
d for a leaflet inviting foreign companies to set up in Brazil? (No more than three.)
e for a postage stamp? (Only one.)

5 Now summarise everything you already know about Brazil – in any form you like.
For example as a spider map, or a poem, or a set of drawings around a map of Brazil.

What's it like?

It's good to know a bit about a country before you visit it!

Brazil's physical features

The Amazon basin and the Brazilian Highlands are Brazil's two main physical features. Look at this map.

The Brazilian Highlands

- ◆ A mix of ancient hills, plateaux (high flat areas) and mountains.
- ◆ They rise sharply from the coast, forming a steep slope called the Great Escarpment.
- ◆ There's just a narrow strip of land between the escarpment and the Atlantic Ocean.

The Amazon

- ◆ Rises in Peru and flows through Brazil to the Atlantic Ocean.
- ◆ The world's second longest river (6577 km). The Nile is first.
- ◆ Has a huge drainage basin (5.8 million square km).
- ◆ Has over 1000 tributaries.
- ◆ Large ships can sail right up it to the border with Peru.

Did you know?
◆ There is not even one bridge over the Amazon, in its 6500 km journey to the ocean.

The coast has many miles of beautiful sandy beaches.

Map

Guyana Highland

River Amazon

Amazon Basin

River Sao Francisco

Brazilian Highlands

Pantanal

River Paraná

0   500 km

N

Rio de Janeiro

Key
height (m)
- 1200 and over
- 800–1200
- 200–800
- 0–200
- - - - edge of drainage basin

Other rivers

- ◆ Brazil has a great many rivers. The map above shows just the main ones. Note their names!
- ◆ The Paraná is the second longest river in South America (4200 km).

Did you know?
◆ Some native Indians believe the Amazon is the moon's tears.
◆ She weeps because she loves the sun but can't get closer to him.

The famous Sugar Loaf mountain above Rio de Janeiro is made of lava. It's the core of an ancient volcano.

Brazil's climate

Most of Brazil lies in the tropics so is hot all year, with an average temperature of around 25 °C. But rainfall varies, due to factors such as:

◆ the height of the land
◆ the distance from the coast
◆ the prevailing wind direction.

So you get different climate zones.

hot with very dry season

◆ hot all year and gets a bit hotter in the dry season
◆ not that much rain in the wet season, and if it fails there is drought.

hot and wet

◆ hot all year – the temperature does not vary much
◆ very wet, with most rain falling in the first half of the year.

a bit cooler, and wet

◆ a bit cooler since it's further from the equator
◆ wet all year but a bit drier towards the middle of the year.

hot and wet, with dry season

◆ quite hot all year (like a hot summer's day in the UK)
◆ has a wet and dry season
◆ most rain falls in December to March when the sun is more directly overhead.

Equator

N

prevailing wind

Tropic of Capricorn

0   500 km

milder and wet

◆ has different seasons, like us
◆ some rain all year round
◆ you may even get snow in winter (around July).

Your turn

1 Which are the two main physical features of Brazil?

2 Write down three facts about the Amazon.

3 This is about the climate map above. (Unit 2.8 and the map on page 100 will help you answer it.)
  a It is always cooler at D than at A. Why?
  b It is always cooler at E than at F. Why?
  c Give a reason why it's wetter at F than at B.
  d C is very close to the equator, and to the Amazon Try to explain why it's always hot and wet there.

4 On the right are four climate graphs. Match them to the four places A–D on the map above.

5 Copy and complete, using words from the list below:
  The _____ _____ of Brazil is _____ and _____.
  The large central area is _____ with a _____ _____.
  The _____ is _____ with four seasons like the UK.
  The driest part of all is in the _____ _____.
  south   hot   north east   wet
  milder   dry season   north west

6 A challenge! When it's winter in London it is summer at D. Explain why. Draw diagrams if that helps.

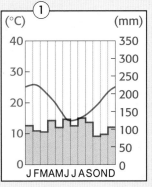

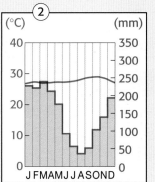

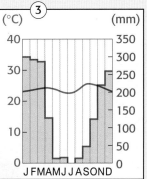

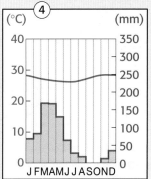

Brazil's natural riches

Brazil is famous for its **biodiversity** – its wide range of plants and animals. It has a wealth of other natural resources too. Lucky Brazil!

Brazil's ecosystems

The tropical rainforest

- The largest area of rainforest in the world. It covers about 40% of Brazil!
- It grows thick and lush.
- It teems with plants, animals and insects. Parrots, monkeys, sloths and orchids just for a start.

Did you know?
- Brazil has over 1600 species of birds.

Equator

N ↑

Tropic of Capricorn

0   500 km

The caatinga

- Semi-arid (like a desert).
- The plants are mainly shrubs and cactus, with very few trees.
- Lots of scorpions, spiders, snakes, and colourful birds live here.

There's a photo of it on page 115.

The Mata Atlantica

- 500 years ago the coast was covered in thick forest. (*Mata* means forest.)
- This had a vast range of trees and plants, including the brasil trees that gave Brazil its name.
- But most of it has been cut down. Only about one tenth is left.

The Pantanal

- The world's largest swampland.
- It's full of water loving plants and animals, including giant anaconda – snakes that can swim.

The cerrado

- This is savanna (as in Unit 3.7).
- In the dry season the grass gets so dry that lightning sets it on fire.
- There are not many trees – and they have thick bark to protect them against fire.
- The animals here include deer, rhea (like ostriches) and wolves.
- You'll see lots of termite mounds like this one.

The pampas

- These are grassy plains.
- Now they are heavily farmed, with many cattle ranches.

Brazil's other natural resources

For centuries the wood in Brazil's forests has been used as a resource. But Brazil has lots of other natural resources too.

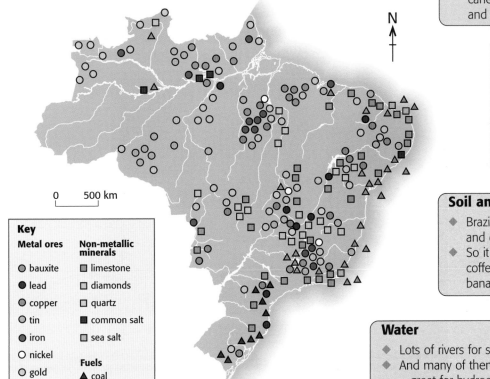

0   500 km

Key

Metal ores	Non-metallic minerals
◐ bauxite	▢ limestone
● lead	▢ diamonds
◕ copper	▢ quartz
◔ tin	◼ common salt
◑ iron	▣ sea salt
○ nickel	**Fuels**
◐ gold	▲ coal
○ zinc	△ oil and gas
	△ nuclear fuels

N ↑

Fuels
- ◆ Brazil has some oil and gas. (But it still needs to import some.)
- ◆ It also grows sugar cane for fuel. Ethanol is made from the sugar cane and burned in car engines and power stations.

Minerals
- ◆ Brazil is a top producer of iron, aluminium, gold, manganese, tin and several other metals …
- ◆ … and of diamonds and other precious stones …
- ◆ … so there are a lot of mines, including some in the rainforest.

Soil and climate
- ◆ Brazil has a wide range of soils – and climates.
- ◆ So it can grow a wide range of crops: coffee, sugar cane, cocoa, rice, bananas, oranges, cotton and more.

Water
- ◆ Lots of rivers for supplying water.
- ◆ And many of them are fast and powerful – great for hydroelectricity (page 70).
- ◆ So Brazil gets 90% of its electricity from hydro. (It has some very large dams!)

Brazil faces one big challenge. How can it exploit its natural resources without harming its ecosystems? Find out about its plans for the rainforest in Unit 7.11.

Your turn

1 a What is an ecosystem? (Unit 3.1 will help.)

  b Name six ecosystems in Brazil and write two sentences about each.

2 Look at the map on page 102.

  a Plants grow really well at X on the map. Why?

  b A cactus can store water in its stem. Explain why cactii have evolved at Y, but are not found at Z. Pages 49 and 101 may help.

3 Why has most of the Mata Atlantica gone? (Clues on pages 104, 106 and 117.)

4 Look at Brazil's other natural resources, above. Which are found in the rainforest? List them.

5 Page 47 showed how we destroy ecosytems in our search for resources.

  a Make a grid like the one on the right, for Brazil.

  b On your grid, mark ✗ where you think two things are in conflict, ✓ where they benefit each other, and O if you think they don't affect each other.

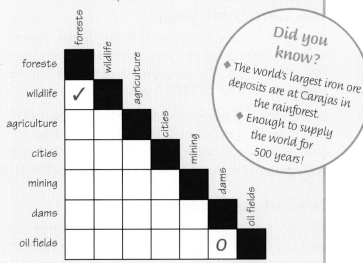

	forests	wildlife	agriculture	cities	mining	dams	oil fields
forests	■						
wildlife	✓	■					
agriculture			■				
cities				■			
mining					■		
dams						■	
oil fields					O		■

Did you know?
- ◆ The world's largest iron ore deposits are at Carajas in the rainforest.
- ◆ Enough to supply the world for 500 years!

The peopling of Brazil

Brazil is a melting pot of different races. How did it get like this?

The Indios

50 000 years ago, the plants and animals had Brazil to themselves. But then at some point – we don't know when – the first humans arrived. They had spread out slowly from East Africa:

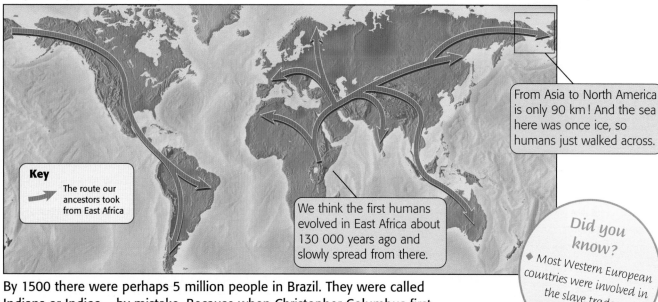

Key
The route our ancestors took from East Africa

From Asia to North America is only 90 km! And the sea here was once ice, so humans just walked across.

We think the first humans evolved in East Africa about 130 000 years ago and slowly spread from there.

By 1500 there were perhaps 5 million people in Brazil. They were called Indians or Indios – by mistake. Because when Christopher Columbus first reached South America, he thought it was India.

The arrival of the Portuguese

On 22 April 1500, a fleet of Portuguese sailing ships arrived at the coast of Brazil. They were led by a nobleman named Pedro Alvarez Cabral. He claimed the land for Portugal.

At first, the Portuguese exported brazilwood from their new colony. Then they switched to sugar cane. Europe was mad about sugar and it grew well in the warm moist climate along the coast.

The slave trade begins

Cutting sugar cane is hard work. At first, Indios were forced to work on the sugar plantations. But they rebelled. Then the Portuguese had another idea. They would 'buy' people in Africa in exchange for cheap goods, and ship them to Brazil to work. It was the start of Europe's **slave trade**.

In 1538 the first slaves arrived. Over the next 300 years at least 4 million African slaves were taken to Brazil. They were forced to work without pay and treated like animals. Many more died at sea in the filthy crowded ships. But at last, in 1888, slavery was abolished in Brazil.

The fortune hunters

By 1700, Brazil's sugar cane industry had begun to decline. And then – gold and diamonds were found. Half a million more Portuguese arrived, hoping to make their fortune. The slaves were put to work in the mines.

Did you know?
◆ Brazil was once a Portuguese colony.
◆ It gained independence in 1822.

Did you know?
◆ Most Western European countries were involved in the slave trade – including Britain.

▲ *The sugar cane harvest.*

Workers from Europe

When slavery ended, Brazil took in workers from Europe. This table shows just the largest groups who came. Most worked on the land. But as towns and cities grew and spread, more workers of all kinds were needed. Like builders, doctors, teachers, engineers, cooks …

Today, you'll find people in Brazil from every race on the Earth.

Immigrants to Brazil, 1876–1976	
Italians	1 600 000
Portuguese	1 500 000
Spanish	600 000
German	300 000
Japanese	250 000

▲ *At a football match in multicultural Brazil.*

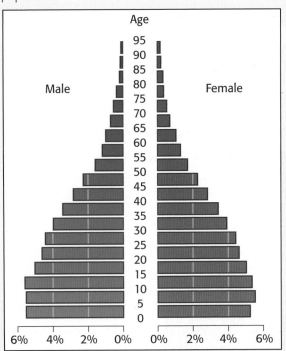

Age

Did you know?
* Brazil once had an emperor.
* Now it's a republic. (No royal family.)

Your turn

1 Explain each of these facts.

a Humans did not reach South America until long after they'd reached North America.

b About 40% of Brazilians are of African descent.

c Brazil is a multicultural society. (Glossary?)

2 Look how Brazil's population has grown:

Year	Brazil's population (millions)
1872	9.9
1900	17.3
1940	41.2
1950	51.9
1960	70.1
1970	93.2
1980	121.3
1991	146.9
2000	172.9
2020	?

a Show this data as a line graph. (Use a full page.)

b In 1960 the population was 70.1 million.

i By about which year had this figure doubled?

ii How many years did it take to double?

iii At this rate, what might it reach in 2020?

3 Its fast population rise means Brazil needs more and more schools. What else does it have to think about? Give your answer as a spider map.

Brazil's population rise means it needs …

more schools   more teachers   more homes

4 A **population pyramid** is a special bar chart that shows ages. Look at this population pyramid for Brazil. It shows that males aged 15–20 form 5% of the population.

a About what % of the population consists of:

i females aged 40–45?   **ii** boys aged 10–15?

iii girls aged 10–15?   **iv** children up to age 5?

b Overall, which is the largest age group?

5 'Brazil is a country of young people'. Do you agree? Give evidence to back up your answer.

So where is everyone?

Today Brazil has over 170 million people. Where do they all live?

Population density

This map shows how people are spread around Brazil. As you can see, some areas have a very high population density and some are almost empty.

Look at the main cities. Rio de Janeiro (*River of January*) is famous. But São Paolo (*Saint Paul*) is larger, with over 16 million people. It is one of the largest cities in the world.

Brasilia is the official capital of Brazil. It was built as a new city and 'opened' in 1960.

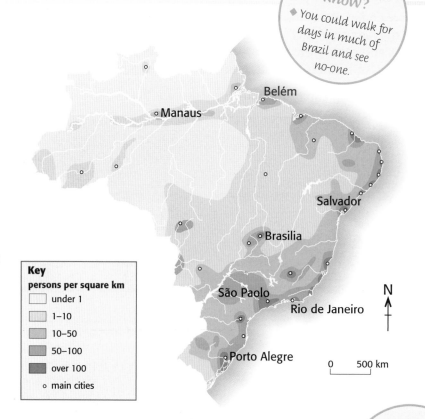

Key
persons per square km
- under 1
- 1–10
- 10–50
- 50–100
- over 100
- ○ main cities

0   500 km

How the cities are growing

Brazil's cities are growing fast. Because people are living longer. Because many Brazilians have large families. And because lots of people from rural areas are moving to the cities, for reasons like these ...

The problems

Life in the city is not all sunshine … especially when people crowd in.

This photo was taken in São Paolo. In front is a **favela** – a settlement of shacks built on waste ground, without permission from anyone. The poorest people in the city live here. It is all they can afford.

Did you know?
- There are nearly 4000 favelas in Brazil.
- Sao Paolo and Rio de Janeiro have most.

Your turn

1. Copy and complete these sentences using words or phrases from the list below. (Check the map!)
   a. The ____ _____ of Brazil is the most crowded part.
   b. Most Brazilians live on or near the ____.
   c. Overall, the rainforest area has ____ ____ people.
   d. The centre of Brazil is quite _____ populated.
   e. The area around São Paolo is ____ populated.
   f. São Paolo is Brazil's _____ city and Rio de Janeiro is _____.

   sparsely   lots of   smallest   very few
   second   north west   south east   densely
   coast   largest

2. Suggest reasons why most Brazilians live on or near the coast. (Think about Brazil's history. The maps on pages 101 and 102 may help too.)

3. a. Look at this table. Compared with the UK:
      i. about many times larger is Brazil in area?
      ii. about how many times larger is its population?
   b. Work out the population density for each country.

4. Today São Paolo is nearly three times larger than it was 30 years ago. Give some reasons for this.

5. You have just moved to São Paolo from a small village, to find work. You have rented a room at X in the favela above. Write a letter to your sister telling her about your new home and its surroundings.

6. Now think about what this person is saying. What will you say in reply?

They should bring the bulldozers in and clear that favela away.

	Brazil	UK
Area (sq km)	8.5 million	0.24 million
Population	173 million	58 million
Population density (number of people per square km)	?	?

How developed is Brazil?

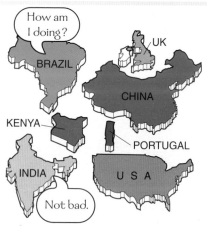

In this area of Brazil people live in shacks, with no running water or electricity.

This place is also in Brazil. It is much more **developed**. You'll find many services provided here.

In the same way you can compare Brazil with other countries to see how developed it is.

What *developed* means

This diagram shows what you'd find in a highly developed country. A good road network and clean modern hospitals, for example.

A **less developed** country may have *some* good roads – and a lot of dirt tracks.

Every country in the world is at a different stage of development. Some are **more developed** than others. Some have a long way to go.

A highly developed country is likely to have …

good roads, a good rail network, many modern factories, comfortable homes, modern airports, electricity everywhere, a supply of clean water piped to homes, a good phone system, clean modern hospitals, good healthcare for everyone, a good supply of food, a good choice when you go shopping, good schools for everyone

How can we measure development?

A highly developed country produces lots of goods and services every year. So one way to measure development is to find the total value of these. This gives the country's **gross domestic product** or **GDP**.

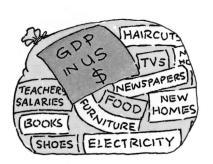

GDP per capita ($US) 1998	
USA	30 000
UK	20 200
Portugal	11 700
Brazil	4500
China	730
India	440
Kenya	330

The **GDP** is the total wealth produced in the country in a year. (It is always given in US dollars.)

GDP per person or **per capita** is the GDP divided by the population of the country.

Usually the more developed the country the higher its GDP per capita, since it is producing a lot.

But GDP per capita does not tell the full story. It does not say *what* the country produces. For example does it produce lots of guns, but not enough school books? Lots of oil, but not enough clean water for everyone?

Other indicators

So to tell how developed a country *really* is, you need to look at other signs or **indicators** *as well as* GDP per capita. Like these:

That's it?

Life expectancy
How many years a new baby in that country can expect to live.

Infant mortality
How many babies per thousand born alive who die before they reach 1.

Adult literacy rate
% of people aged 15 and over who can read and write a simple sentence.

Daily calorie supply
How much a person there gets to eat per day, on average, in calories.

Your turn

1 Do you think *you* live in a highly developed country? Give reasons.

2 Draw a diagram like the one on page 108 to show what you'd expect to find in a less developed country. (For example *not enough hospitals, not enough schools*.)

3 a What does *GDP per capita* mean?
  b Draw a bar graph to show the data for GDP per capita from page 108.
  c Now, using your graph to help you, write a paragraph comparing Brazil to the other countries.

4 a What does *life expectancy* mean?
  b As a country develops, life expectancy rises. Why? Suggest as many reasons as you can. Give your answer as a spider map, like this:

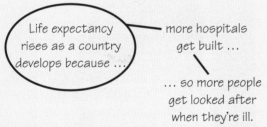

Life expectancy rises as a country develops because ...

more hospitals get built ...

... so more people get looked after when they're ill.

5 Now look at the other three indicators at the top of this page. For each, say whether it will *rise* or *fall* as the country develops, and give one reason.

6

Changes in Brazil		
Indicator	**1970**	**1998**
GDP per capita ($ US)	3200	4500
Life expectancy (years)	60	67
Infant mortality (per 1000 babies)	95	36
Adult literacy rate, %	66	85
Daily calorie supply	2410	2970

Look at the table above. Is Brazil growing more developed, less developed or staying the same? Give data to support your answer.

7 Now look at the table at the bottom of the page.
  a Using this data, see if you can put the 7 countries in order, with the most developed one first. (Perhaps you could rank each country from 1 to 7 for each indicator, then add up its rank numbers?)
  b Compare your list with the list for *GDP per capita* on page 108. Is Brazil in the same place in each?

8 So far you have met five indicators of development. There are many others! Decide if this could be used as an indicator, and say why:
  a the amount of electricity used per person
  b the number of cars per thousand people
  c the % of the population with access to the Internet
  d how happy the people feel.

Country	Life expectancy (years)	Infant mortality per 1000 babies	Adult literacy rate (%)	Daily calorie supply (calories)
Brazil	67	36	85	2970
China	70	38	83	2900
India	63	69	56	2500
Kenya	51	75	81	1980
Portugal	76	8	91	3670
UK	77	6	99	3280
USA	77	7	99	3700

Inequality in Brazil

Barbra and Pedro are both 14. They both live in Rio de Janeiro. And worlds apart …

Barbra's day

My mum woke me as usual at 6 am – groan. Coconut pancakes and orange juice for breakfast. Then dad's driver drove me to school for 7. We had Miss Cardoso today – boring! When school finished at 12 we had dance class for an hour. We do all kinds of modern dance.

Magaretta's mother drove us home, and we got my mum and my two brothers and went to the beach. We do that two or three times a week. We joined in a game of volleyball for a while, and swam. Magaretta and I read magazines.

After the beach, homework for an hour. Then dad came home from the office and we had dinner. Lucia is our cook and she cooked feijoada today. It's a bean and pork stew. Now I'm going to watch a game show on TV, then have a bath and go to bed. But first I want mum to promise to take me shopping for clothes tomorrow. It's Saturday and I have to go to Anita's party.

Pedro's day

I always wake at 5 am. You can't sleep late in our house – not with all seven of us in one room and the baby crying! I grabbed my bucket and sponge and ran. It's about 3 km to our junction.

Francesco was already there and traffic was busy. So I filled my bucket at the petrol station tap and got started. You have to be fast washing windscreens at the traffic lights – they don't stay on red that long.

Most of the drivers are okay. But some are really nasty – they wait till you finish and then grin and drive off without giving you any money.

At 11 we took a break. We went to the market and bought bread and soup. We ate on the corner as usual. Francesco went on as usual about getting a proper job. He says there are classes to teach poor people like us how to use computers, and we should try to get into one.

We'll stay at the junction until it's dark and most people have gone home from work. Then I'll run home really fast. I'm always worried a gang will attack me and steal my money. Or that I'll fall into a drain and ruin my only pair of jeans!

I make about 6 reais a day. (*About £2.20.*) When I get home I'll give most of it to my mother – she has to pay the rent on Friday. Then we'll have bean stew, as usual. And then I'll crash out. Tomorrow is another busy day.

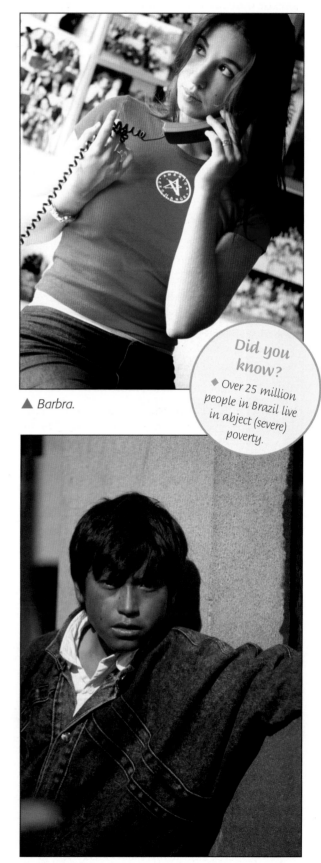

▲ Barbra.

▲ Pedro.

Did you know?
◆ Over 25 million people in Brazil live in abject (severe) poverty.

An unequal society

If all the wealth produced in a year in Brazil were shared out equally, everyone would get about 2000 US dollars a year. (That's about £1340).

But it is not shared equally. Some Brazilians are very wealthy. But over a third of the population live on under US $700 a year. (About £470.)

There is **inequality** in every society. Some people have plenty of everything, and many have almost nothing. It is a big problem in Brazil.

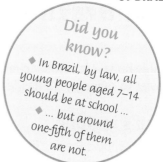

Did you know?
- In Brazil, by law, all young people aged 7–14 should be at school ...
- ... but around one-fifth of them are not.

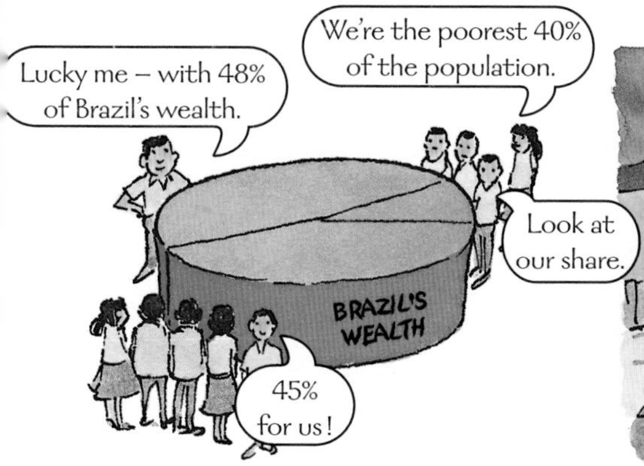
Lucky me – with 48% of Brazil's wealth.
We're the poorest 40% of the population.
Look at our share.
BRAZIL'S WEALTH
45% for us!

Each person here represents 10% of Brazil's population.
48% of Brazil's wealth is owned by just 10% of the people!

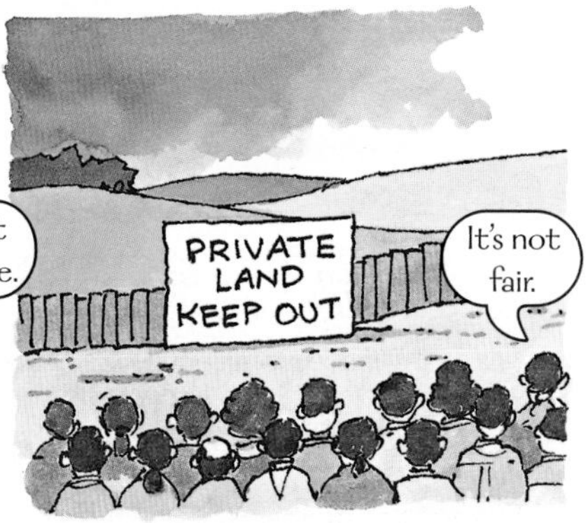
PRIVATE LAND KEEP OUT
It's not fair.

Less than 3% of the population owns two thirds of the farmland – and nearly 5 million rural families have no land at all.

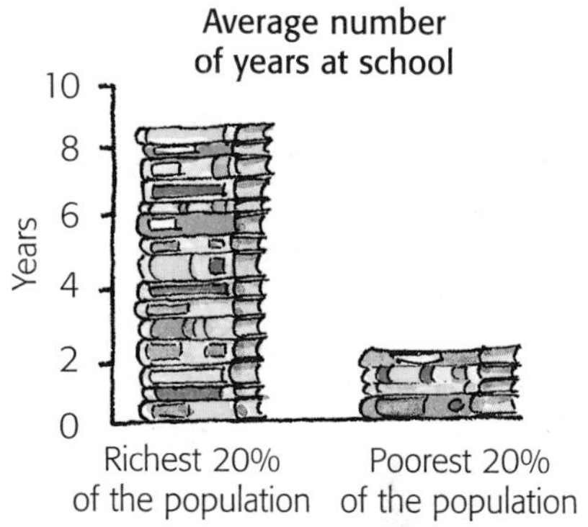
Average number of years at school
Years
0
2
4
6
8
10
Richest 20% of the population
Poorest 20% of the population

Poor people in Brazil are likely to have very little education – which means they have less chance of improving their lives.

Here is one reason for the inequality. Portuguese kings used to give out huge tracts of land in Brazil as rewards and gifts to people. The new landowners got slaves to work on the land at first, for no pay. Then they hired European workers and paid them very little.

Today the landowners' families still own the land, and have got richer and richer. The descendants of their slaves and workers have not.

Did you know?
- 90% of professional footballers in Brazil earn about £90 a month.

Your turn

1 Make a large table to compare Barbra and Pedro's day. You could do it like this:

	Barbra	Pedro
morning	breakfast of ...	

2 *Why* has Barbra ended up with a more comfortable life than Pedro? Try to suggest some reasons.

3 Compare these pie charts for Brazil and the UK.

How wealth is distributed

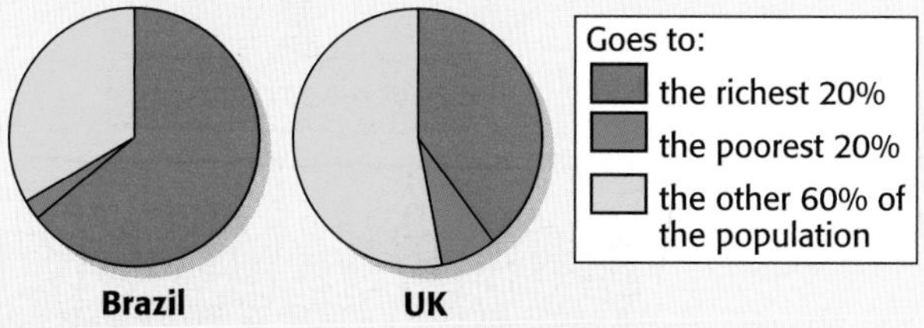
Goes to:
the richest 20%
the poorest 20%
the other 60% of the population
Brazil
UK

a Is there inequality in the UK? Explain.
b Which has a more unequal society, Brazil or the UK?

4 The government wants to make Brazil a more equal society. Here are two of the things it plans.

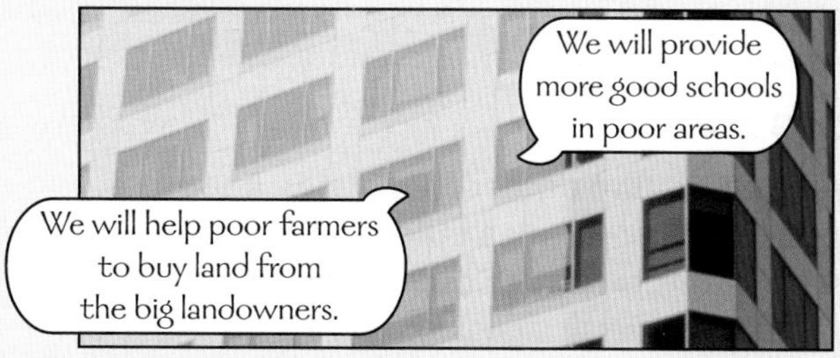
We will provide more good schools in poor areas.
We will help poor farmers to buy land from the big landowners.

Draw a flow chart to show how each will help to reduce inequality. You could start the first one like this. (Then think about how the farmers could use the money they earn.)

Poor farmers without land get help to buy some.
↓
Now they can grow food to feed their families.
↓
They can grow extra food to sell.

How Brazil is divided up

Brazil is huge – it would cover about 85% of Europe. To make it easier to manage, it's divided up into regions and states.

Brazil's regions

This map shows Brazil's five **regions**: North, South, North East, South East and West Central.

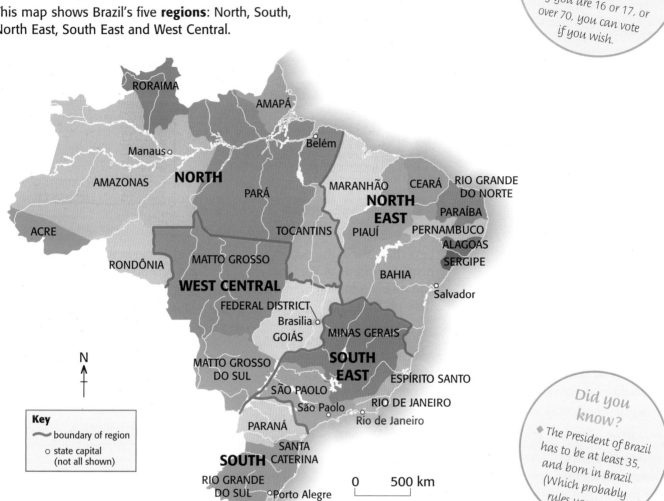

Key
~ boundary of region
o state capital (not all shown)

0   500 km

Brazil's states

Each region is in turn divided into **states**. There are 26 states plus a special area called the **federal district**. Each state has its own state capital. The federal district has Brasilia, the overall capital of Brazil.

So who's in charge?

Each state is run by a state government, led by a governor. But above them all is the **federal government**, based in Brasilia. It is led by the president of Brazil.

The federal government makes big decisions for the whole country. For example about road networks, and how to defend the country. State governments must do what the federal government decides.

▲ *Brazil's flag.*

◄ *Brasilia, the federal capital of Brazil. It's famous for its modern buildings. Note the favela too.*

Your turn

Region of Brazil	Average number of people per square km	% of the total GDP it contributes	% of children in urban areas who *don't* go to school	% of homes in urban areas *without* a water supply
North	2.9	4.4	7.9	30.9
South	39.5	17.1	5.3	5.1
North East	28.3	13.8	9.5	13.9
South East	70.1	59.4	4.7	4.5
West Central	6.1	5.3	5.2	17.3

1 To answer this question you will need the maps on pages 112, 102, 101 and 98. Which region of Brazil:
   a is largest?
   b is smallest?
   c does the Amazon river flow through?
   d is almost all rainforest?
   e probably has most beaches?
   f has an area that suffers drought?
   g gets most rainfall?
   h is home to the Pantanal?
   i does the equator run through?
   j lies outside the tropics?
   k is home to the federal government?

2 This is about the states and capitals. Name:
   a the largest state
   b three states that are mainly rainforest
   c two states with the same name as their capitals
   d the most southern state
   e the most western state
   f two states the Amazon river runs through
   g the state capital at the mouth of the Amazon
   h the official capital of Brazil.

3 There are many differences between Brazil's regions. Look at the table above.
   a Which region is the most densely populated?
   b Which produces most goods and services?
   c Which is *most successful* at providing a water supply to urban homes? (Careful!)

4 The table shows three indicators of development.
   a For each indicator, list the states in order with *the most successful one* first.
   b Now compare your three lists. Overall, which region of Brazil do you think is:
     i most developed?
     ii least developed? See if you can suggest a reason why it is least developed.

5 Now look at Brazil's flag.
   a What do you think the stars represent? (You could try counting them!)
   b What does the upper star represent?
   c What do you think the white band around the middle of the globe represents?
   d Why do you think they chose those colours for the flag? Think of some sensible suggestions.

Comparing two regions

It's time to practice being a geography detective!

You have to compare two of Brazil's regions, the North East and South East. You'll find lots of clues on these two pages.

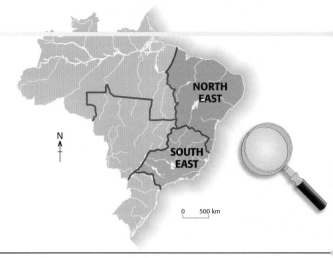

1 Relief and climate

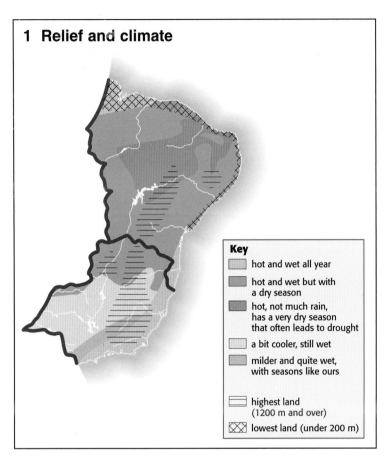

Key

- hot and wet all year
- hot and wet but with a dry season
- hot, not much rain, has a very dry season that often leads to drought
- a bit cooler, still wet
- milder and quite wet, with seasons like ours

- highest land (1200 m and over)
- lowest land (under 200 m)

2 Population density

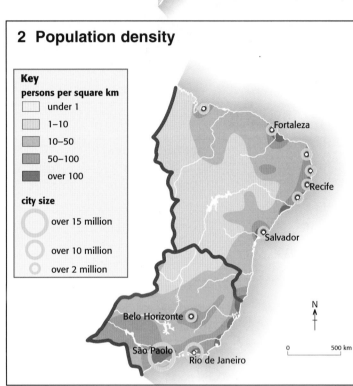

Key

persons per square km
- under 1
- 1–10
- 10–50
- 50–100
- over 100

city size
- over 15 million
- over 10 million
- over 2 million

Fortaleza
Recife
Salvador
Belo Horizonte
São Paolo
Rio de Janeiro

4 Economic activity

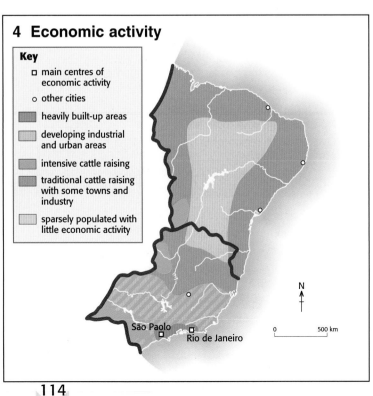

Key

- □ main centres of economic activity
- ○ other cities
- heavily built-up areas
- developing industrial and urban areas
- intensive cattle raising
- traditional cattle raising with some towns and industry
- sparsely populated with little economic activity

São Paolo
Rio de Janeiro

3 Resources

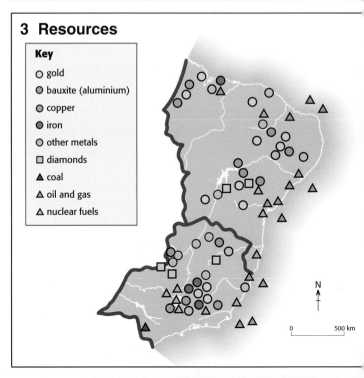

Key

- ○ gold
- ○ bauxite (aluminium)
- ○ copper
- ○ iron
- ○ other metals
- □ diamonds
- ▲ coal
- △ oil and gas
- △ nuclear fuels

▲ Farmland in the South East region.

▲ A small farm in the caatinga in North East region.

Some social indicators	South East	North East
% of households with electricity	98	78
% of urban households with public water supply	99.5	86.1
% of children in urban areas not attending school	4.7	9.5
% of urban households with a fixed line phone	34.9	20.0
% of households with TV	95	83.8

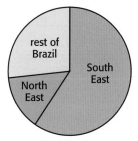

Contribution to GDP

Your turn

1 First, make a copy of this table. Then fill in a tick in the correct column. (You might need to tick both!) One has been done for you.

	NE	SE
Has more high land		✔
Has Brazil's largest cities		
Is more crowded, overall		
Gets more rain, overall		
Often suffers drought		
Has a better climate for farming		
Has lots of mineral resources		
Has oil, gas and diamonds		
Is richer in iron, which Brazil needs to make steel for buildings, bridges, cars and many other things		
Has more industry		
Produces most of Brazil's goods and services		
Is more developed		

2 The two photos above show farming areas.
 a The first shows *intensive* farming.
   What do you think that means?
 b Describe the differences you see in the two areas.
 c Suggest one big reason why they look so different.

3 A and B below describe two regions. But which is which? Match each to the correct region.

> **A**
> This is the economic core of Brazil. It covers only 11% of the area of Brazil, but has 44% of the workforce. It has lots of factories. It provides more jobs in manufacturing than any other region. Overall, the workers here are better paid than in other regions.

> **B**
> This covers 18% of Brazil's area, but has only 4% of its workforce. To help it, the government has given big grants to industries to set up factories here. Some have done very well. But they use machines rather than people so have not created many new jobs.

4 A good detective gathers clues, and then comes up with explanations!
 Now *you* have to try to explain why the South East of Brazil is so much more developed than the North East. You can give your answer in any form you choose. For example as a strip cartoon, or a written report, or a flow chart, or a spider map, or an interview with a politician.

Brazil's place in the world

Every country depends to some extent on other countries.
Countries are **interdependent**. Just look at Brazil!

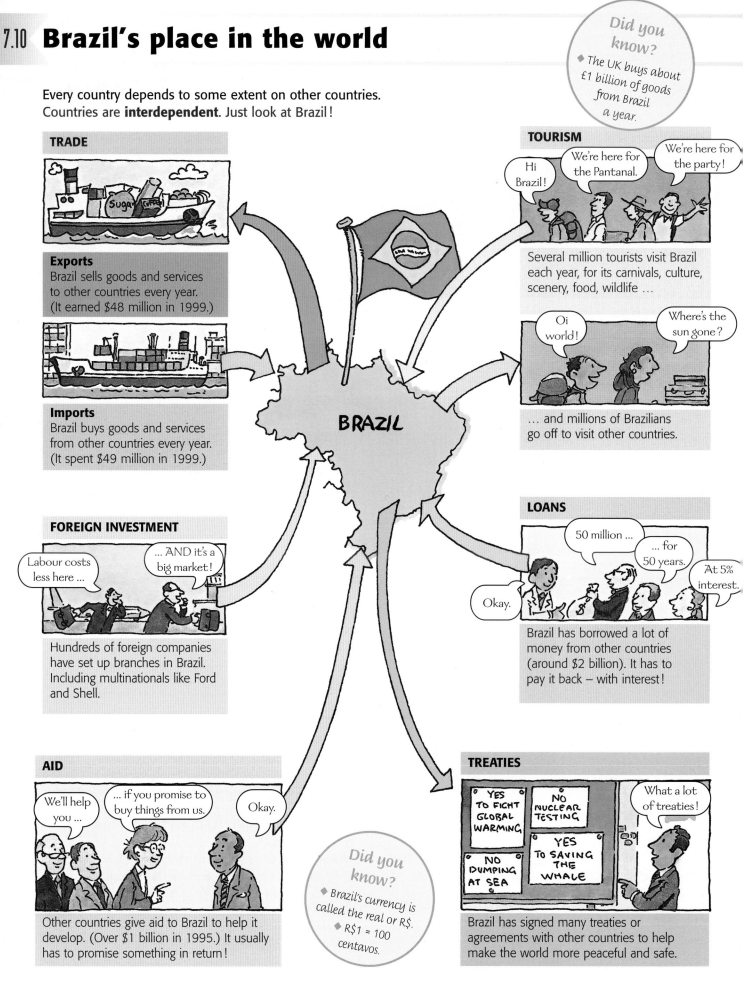

TRADE

Exports
Brazil sells goods and services to other countries every year.
(It earned $48 million in 1999.)

Imports
Brazil buys goods and services from other countries every year.
(It spent $49 million in 1999.)

FOREIGN INVESTMENT

Labour costs less here ...

... AND it's a big market!

Hundreds of foreign companies have set up branches in Brazil.
Including multinationals like Ford and Shell.

AID

We'll help you ...

... if you promise to buy things from us.

Okay.

Other countries give aid to Brazil to help it develop. (Over $1 billion in 1995.) It usually has to promise something in return!

TOURISM

Hi Brazil!

We're here for the Pantanal.

We're here for the party!

Several million tourists visit Brazil each year, for its carnivals, culture, scenery, food, wildlife ...

Oi world!

Where's the sun gone?

... and millions of Brazilians go off to visit other countries.

LOANS

50 million ...

... for 50 years.

At 5% interest.

Okay.

Brazil has borrowed a lot of money from other countries (around $2 billion). It has to pay it back – with interest!

TREATIES

YES TO FIGHT GLOBAL WARMING

NO NUCLEAR TESTING

YES TO SAVING THE WHALE

NO DUMPING AT SEA

What a lot of treaties!

Brazil has signed many treaties or agreements with other countries to help make the world more peaceful and safe.

BRAZIL

The importance of trade to Brazil

Ever since the Portuguese arrived in 1500, trade has been important to Brazil. For hundreds of years it depended on different 'star' exports for a living. Look at this graph:

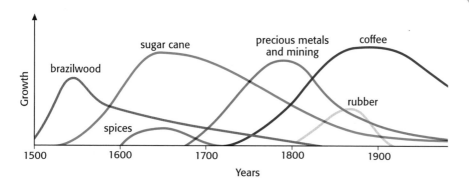

But it's dangerous to depend too much on just a few exports. As the graph shows, all exports decline in the end! A product may go out of fashion. Or another country may start to sell it more cheaply. (This is what happened with rubber.)

Meanwhile, for hundreds of years, Brazil imported machinery and other goods it needed. They cost a fortune. So it decided to *make* them instead of importing them. This is called **import substitution**.

The plan worked well. As you'll see below, Brazil now exports more **manufactured products** than **primary products**.

▲ *Brazil makes millions of cars for export.*

Your turn

1 Countries are *interdependent*. What does that mean?

2 List six ways Brazil depends on other countries. ('To buy its goods' is one.)

3 Look at the pie chart below.
   a What do you think *primary products* are? Give two examples.
   b What does *manufactured products* mean?
   c Some of the goods Brazil exports are called *semi-manufactured*. Leather is an example. Why are they called this?

Brazil's exports, 1999

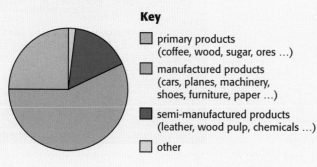

Key
- ▨ primary products (coffee, wood, sugar, ores ...)
- ▨ manufactured products (cars, planes, machinery, shoes, furniture, paper ...)
- ▨ semi-manufactured products (leather, wood pulp, chemicals ...)
- ☐ other

4 In 1999, Brazil exported goods worth US$ 48 million. It imported goods worth US$ 49 million.
   a So it spent more than it earned. How much more?
   b If it kept spending more than it earned, would that be good or bad? Draw a spider map like the one started here, to show why.

If Brazil keeps on spending more than it earns, it means ..

less money for schools, so ...

less money for hospitals, so ...

   c Which is wiser to import: clothes or machinery? Why?

5 Brazil does not attract as many tourists as it could. You are the Minister of Tourism. Write a report for the President of Brazil, saying:
   a why Brazil has a lot to offer tourists
   b why it's important to attract more tourists
   c what steps you will take to attract more tourists.

The rainforest challenge

For centuries, Brazil's rainforest lay scarcely disturbed. But in 1965 a new highway was built from Belém, through the rainforest, to Brasilia. And soon logging and mining companies, ranchers, farmers and hunters moved in.

Since then, large areas have been **deforested**. (See the photos on page 53.) This has caused conflict both inside and outside Brazil …

Taking up the challenge

Brazil's government has thought hard about all these demands. It still plans to exploit the rainforest – but **sustainably**. Like this:

> **SUSTAINABLE DEVELOPMENT IN THE RAINFOREST**
>
> ◆ Mining companies must reforest the area when a mine is exhausted.
>
> ◆ Logging companies may cut down trees in only certain areas – and should plant new ones to replace them.
>
> ◆ We will have **extractive reserves** – areas where people can carry out sustainable activities such as spice growing and rubber tapping.
>
> ◆ We will allow small factories that make goods from rainforest materials. For example salad oil and Brazil cake from Brazil nuts. This will create jobs for people living in the rainforest region.
>
> ◆ The rights of the Indios must be protected.
>
> ◆ Large parts of the rainforest must be left undisturbed.

But the government also intends to build new highways through the rainforest. Because of this, many people are still worried that most of it will be destroyed in the end.

▲ *Mining for iron ore at Carajas in the rainforest..*

▲ *Rubber tapping is sustainable. The rubber is taken from the living tree.*

▲ *A small factory in the rainforest making…?*

A life-saving future?

There's one way Brazil can use the rainforest to help everyone – for medicine! For centuries the Indians have used rainforest plants to cure diseases. Now scientists think that as many as 300 life-saving drugs may lie hidden in the rainforest plants.

Drug companies can study a healing plant to find the key ingredient. Then they can 'copy' this in a factory. New drugs from rainforest plants could earn them billions of pounds.

Some drug companies learn all they can about a plant from the Indians, and then take it away and **patent** the healing substance so that they 'own' it by law. This kind of stealing is called **biopiracy**. Brazil is now fighting the biopirates, to get a fair share of the money from new drugs.

Did you know?
◆ 125 foreign drug companies have offices in Brazil. (And the rainforest is one reason …)

Did you know?
◆ Only about 1% of the world's plants have been studied so far, for medical use.

Did you know?
◆ Most of the world's top medical drugs are derived from plants and animals.

Your turn

1 List all the activities that are damaging the world's rainforests. (Page 52 will help.)

2 Many groups want a say in the future of Brazil's rainforest. But who are they? Match each group on page 118 to one of these labels:

Foreign companies	The World Bank
Brazil's rural poor	Environmental groups such as Greenpeace
The Brazilian government	
Governments of other countries	The Indios

3 Of all the groups on page 118, whose side will you take? Choose just one group, and explain why you've chosen it.

4 Some of the groups above are more powerful than others, so have more influence on the Brazilian government. See if you can arrange them in order, with the most powerful one first. Give reasons for your choice.

5 The Brazilian government feels it must earn *something* from the rainforest, to help Brazil.
   a List all the resources in Brazil's rainforest that could be exploited. (Unit 7.3 will help.)
   b The government wants to exploit the rainforest in a *sustainable* way. What does that mean?

6 What do these mean? The glossary may help.
   a to patent something   b biopiracy

7 This is José, an Indian from the Macuxi tribe.

A drug company has visited his tribe and taken samples of all their healing plants. José can't write. So you must write a letter to the drug company for him. Say that if they make drugs from these plants, his tribe has a right to a share of the earnings – and give reasons.

Ordnance Survey symbols

ROADS AND PATHS

Not necessarily rights of way

Service area M 8 Elevated	Motorway (dual carriageway)
Junction number	
	Motorway under construction
Unfenced Footbridge	Trunk road
A 92 (T)	
Dual carriageway	Main road
A 917	
	Main road under construction
	Secondary road
B 9131	
	Narrow road with passing places
A 855 B 885	
Bridge	Road generally more than 4 m wide
	Road generally less than 4 m wide
	Other road, drive or track
	Path
Gates Road tunnel	
Ferry P Ferry V	
Ferry (passenger) Ferry (vehicle)	

PUBLIC RIGHTS OF WAY

(Not applicable to Scotland)

··············	Footpath	– – – – –	Road used as a public footpath
– – – – –	Bridleway	+–+–+–+–	Byway open to all traffic

RAILWAYS

	Track multiple or single	+—+—+	Freight line, siding or tramway
	Track narrow gauge	a b	Station (a) principal (b) closed to passengers
	Bridges, Footbridge		
	Tunnel	LC	Level crossing
	Viaduct		Embankment
			Cutting

BOUNDARIES

–·–+–·+	National	–·–·–·–·	County, Region or Islands Area
–·–·–·–	London Borough	–·+–·+	District
	National Park or Forest Park		
NT	National Trust	NT	always open
		NT	limited access, observe local signs

GENERAL FEATURES

	Electricity transmission line (with pylons spaced conventionally)		Quarry
>–·>–·>	Pipe line (arrow indicates direction of flow)		Spoil heap, refuse tip or dump
ruin	Buildings		Radio or TV mast
	Public buildings (selected)		Places of Worship { with tower
	Bus or coach station		with spire, minaret or dome
	Coniferous wood		without such additions
	Non-coniferous wood	°	Chimney or tower
	Mixed wood		Glasshouse
	Orchard	+	Graticule intersection at 5' intervals
	Park or ornamental grounds	H	Heliport
		△	Triangulation pillar
			Windmill with or without sails
			Windpump/wind generator

HEIGHTS/ROCK FEATURES

50	Contours are at 10 metres vertical interval
·144	Heights are to the nearest metre above mean sea level

outcrop   cliff   scree

WATER FEATURES

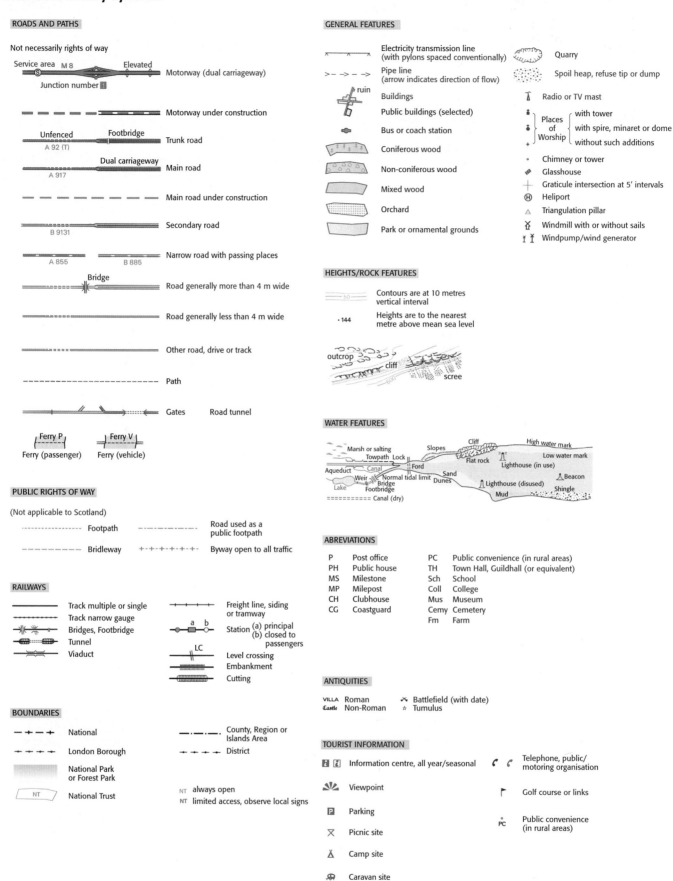

Marsh or salting · Towpath Lock · Cliff · High water mark · Slopes · Flat rock · Low water mark · Aqueduct · Canal · Ford · Lighthouse (in use) · Weir · Normal tidal limit · Sand · Beacon · Bridge · Dunes · Lighthouse (disused) · Shingle · Lake · Footbridge · Mud

========= Canal (dry)

ABREVIATIONS

P	Post office	PC	Public convenience (in rural areas)
PH	Public house	TH	Town Hall, Guildhall (or equivalent)
MS	Milestone	Sch	School
MP	Milepost	Coll	College
CH	Clubhouse	Mus	Museum
CG	Coastguard	Cemy	Cemetery
		Fm	Farm

ANTIQUITIES

VILLA	Roman		Battlefield (with date)
Castle	Non-Roman	☆	Tumulus

TOURIST INFORMATION

	Information centre, all year/seasonal		Telephone, public/ motoring organisation
	Viewpoint		Golf course or links
P	Parking		
✕	Picnic site	PC	Public convenience (in rural areas)
⋏	Camp site		
	Caravan site		
▲	Youth hostel		

120

Map of the British Isles

Key

- – – – – international boundary
- —— national boundary
- ～～ river
- lake
- ▲ highest point in the UK

towns
- ■ largest cities
- ● large cities and towns

Land height
measured in metres above sea level

- more than 1000 m
- 500 - 1000 m
- 200 - 500 m
- 100 - 200 m
- less than 100 m
- land below sea level

Scale

1: 4 500 000

One centimetre on the map represents
45 kilometres on the ground.

0   45   90   135   180 km

Transverse Mercator Projection

Shetland Islands

Orkney Islands

Cape Wrath

Outer Hebrides

Lewis

NORTHWEST HIGHLANDS

Skye

Great Glen

Loch Ness

River Spey

CAIRNGORMS

River Dee

● Aberdeen

1344m ▲ Ben Nevis

GRAMPIAN MOUNTAINS

Mull

R. Tay

SCOTLAND

● Dundee

Loch Lomond

Firth of Forth

Islay

Glasgow ●

River Clyde

● Edinburgh

Firth of Clyde

SOUTHERN UPLANDS

R. Tweed

UNITED KINGDOM

CHEVIOT HILLS

North Channel

NORTHERN IRELAND

R. Bann

ANTRIM MOUNTAINS

River Tyne

Newcastle upon Tyne ●

● Sunderland

River Eden

River Tees

Stockton-on-Tees ●

Middlesbrough ●

River Erne

Lough Neagh

● Belfast

LAKE DISTRICT

PENNINES

NORTH YORK MOORS

River Ouse

REPUBLIC OF IRELAND

Lough Corrib

Isle of Man

NORTH ATLANTIC OCEAN

Irish Sea

Blackpool ●

Preston ●

Bradford ● Leeds ●

Kingston-upon-Hull ●

Huddersfield ●

River Aire

R. Boyne

Bolton ● Manchester ●

River Humber

R. Liffey

● Dublin

Anglesey

Liverpool ●

Stockport ●

River Shannon

River Barrow

Warrington ●

River Mersey

Sheffield ●

WICKLOW MOUNTAINS

ENGLAND

Stoke-on-Trent ●

R. Dee

Derby ●

River Suir

River Blackwater

CAMBRIAN MOUNTAINS

R. Dee

Nottingham ●

The Wash

R. Wensum

● Cork

Cardigan Bay

River Severn

Telford ●

R. Trent

Leicester ●

THE FENS

Peterborough ●

Norwich ●

Walsall ●

Wolverhampton ●

■ Birmingham

Coventry ●

Northampton ●

R. Great Ouse

St George's Channel

WALES

Dudley ●

Solihull ●

Ipswich ●

River Teifi

River Usk

R. Wye

River Avon

Milton Keynes ●

R. Stour

River Tywi

BRECON BEACONS

Luton ●

CHILTERN HILLS

Swansea ●

Newport ●

COTSWOLD HILLS

R. Thames

Basildon ●

Southend-on-Sea ●

Cardiff ●

Reading ●

■ London

Bristol ●

NORTH DOWNS

NORTH ATLANTIC OCEAN

Bristol Channel

SALISBURY PLAIN

SOUTH DOWNS

EXMOOR

Southampton ●

Bournemouth ●

Portsmouth ● Brighton ●

R. Exe

Poole ●

DARTMOOR

Isle of Wight

Torbay ●

Land's End

Plymouth ●

Strait of Dover

Isles of Scilly

English Channel

North Sea

121

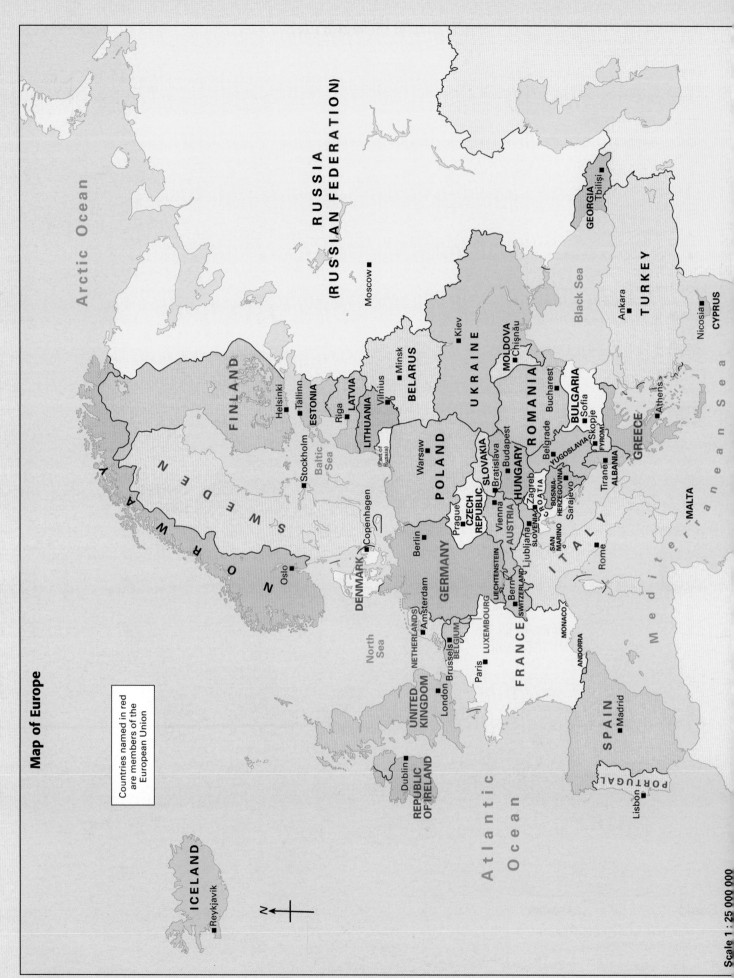

Map of Europe

Countries named in red are members of the European Union

122

Scale 1 : 25 000 000

N

Arctic Ocean

Atlantic Ocean

ICELAND
■ Reykjavik

NORWAY
Oslo ■

SWEDEN
Stockholm ■

FINLAND
Helsinki ■

RUSSIA
(RUSSIAN FEDERATION)

Moscow ■

ESTONIA
■ Tallinn

LATVIA
Riga ■

Baltic Sea

LITHUANIA
Vilnius ■

(Part of Russia)

BELARUS
Minsk ■

UKRAINE
Kiev ■

DENMARK
Copenhagen ■

North Sea

REPUBLIC OF IRELAND
Dublin ■

UNITED KINGDOM
London ■

NETHERLANDS
Amsterdam ■

BELGIUM
Brussels ■

GERMANY
Berlin ■

POLAND
Warsaw ■

CZECH REPUBLIC
Prague ■

SLOVAKIA
Bratislava ■

AUSTRIA
Vienna ■

HUNGARY
Budapest ■

MOLDOVA
Chişnău ■

ROMANIA
Bucharest ■

LUXEMBOURG

FRANCE
Paris ■

LIECHTENSTEIN

SWITZERLAND
Bern ■

SLOVENIA
Ljubljana ■

CROATIA
Zagreb ■

BOSNIA-HERZEGOVINA
Sarajevo ■

YUGOSLAVIA
Belgrade ■

BULGARIA
Sofia ■

FYROM
Skopje ■

ALBANIA
Tiranë ■

GREECE
Athens ■

MONACO

ANDORRA

SAN MARINO

ITALY
Rome ■

MALTA

SPAIN
Madrid ■

PORTUGAL
Lisbon ■

Mediterranean Sea

Black Sea

GEORGIA
Tbilisi ■

TURKEY
Ankara ■

CYPRUS
Nicosia ■

Map of the world (physical)

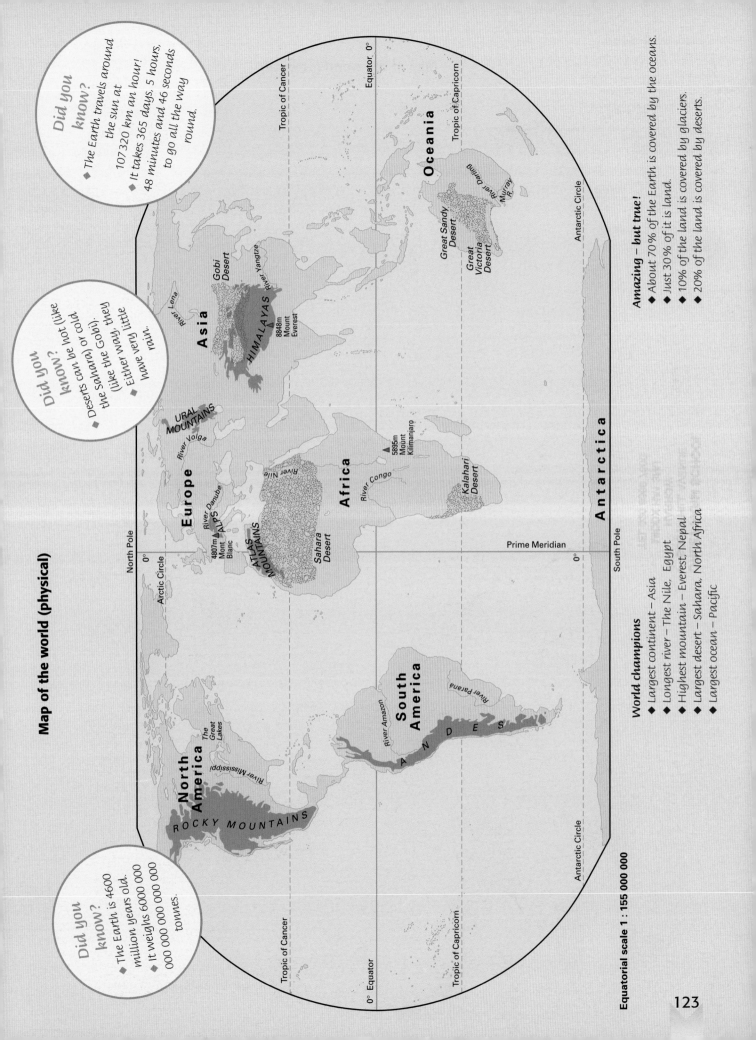

Amazing – but true!
- About 70% of the Earth is covered by the oceans.
- Just 30% of it is land.
- 10% of the land is covered by glaciers.
- 20% of the land is covered by deserts.

World champions
- Largest continent – Asia
- Longest river – The Nile, Egypt
- Highest mountain – Everest, Nepal
- Largest desert – Sahara, North Africa
- Largest ocean – Pacific

Equatorial scale 1 : 155 000 000

Legend

— international boundary
• capital city

abbreviations
BELG.	BELGIUM
B-H.	BOSNIA-HERZEGOVINA
C.	CROATIA
CENT. AF. REP.	CENTRAL AFRICAN REPUBLIC
CZ.	CZECH REPUBLIC
F.	FYROM
	(Former Yugoslav Republic of Macedonia)
L.	LIECHTENSTEIN
LITH.	LITHUANIA
LUX.	LUXEMBOURG
NETH.	NETHERLANDS
S.	SLOVENIA
SL.	SLOVAKIA
SWITZ.	SWITZERLAND
U.A.E.	UNITED ARAB EMIRATES
U.S.A.	UNITED STATES OF AMERICA
Y.	YUGOSLAVIA

Equatorial Scale 1: 95 000 000

Did you know?
◆ Greenland has the world's lowest population density – 0.04 people per sq km.
◆ Monaco has the highest – 17 203 people per sq km.

ORLEY FARM SCHOOL
SOUTH HILL AVENUE
HARROW
MIDDX HA1 3NU
TEL 020 8869 7600

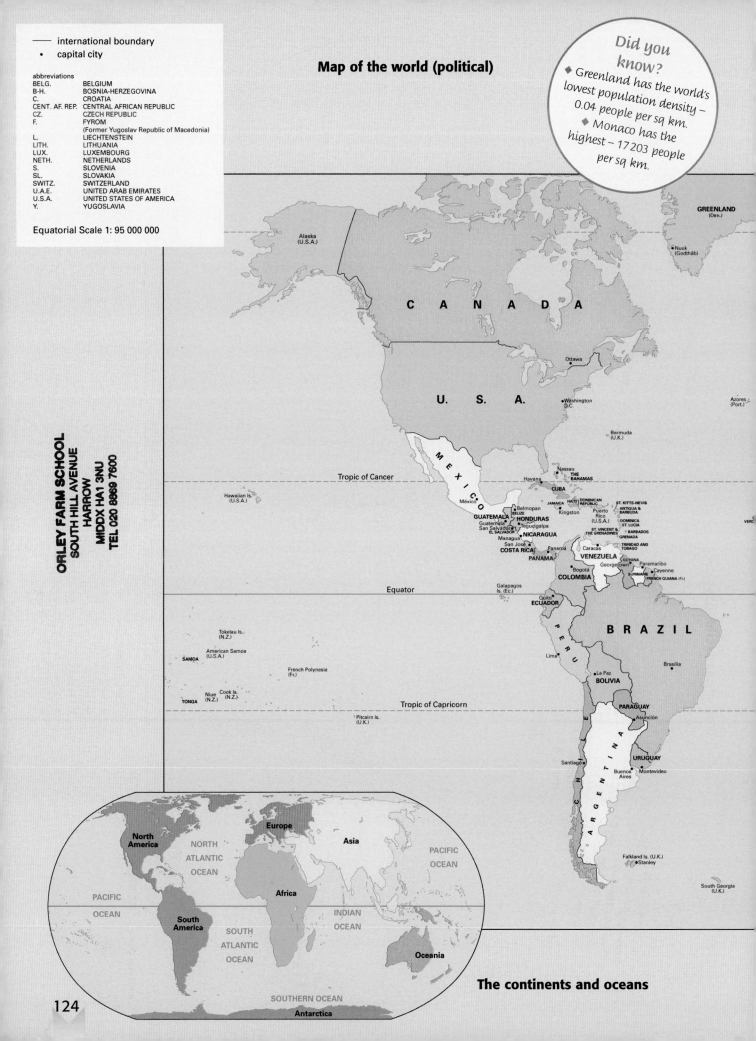

GREENLAND
(Den.)

Nuuk
(Godthåb)

Alaska
(U.S.A.)

C A N A D A

Ottawa

U. S. A.

•Washington
D.C.

Azores
(Port.)

Bermuda
(U.K.)

Tropic of Cancer

Hawaiian Is.
(U.S.A.)

MEXICO

México

Nassau
THE
BAHAMAS

Havana

CUBA

JAMAICA HAITI DOMINICAN
REPUBLIC

ST. KITTS-NEVIS
ANTIGUA &
BARBUDA

Belmopan
BELIZE

Kingston Puerto
Rico
(U.S.A.)

DOMINICA
ST. LUCIA

GUATEMALA HONDURAS

Guatemala Tegucigalpa
San Salvador
EL SALVADOR NICARAGUA

ST. VINCENT &
THE GRENADINES BARBADOS
GRENADA

Managua

San José
COSTA RICA Panamá
PANAMA

TRINIDAD AND
TOBAGO

Caracas
VENEZUELA

GUYANA Paramaribo
Georgetown SURINAME Cayenne
FRENCH GUIANA (Fr.)

VER

Bogotá
COLOMBIA

Galapagos
Is. (Ec.)

Equator

Quito
ECUADOR

P
E
R
U

B R A Z I L

Lima

Brasília

La Paz
BOLIVIA

Tokelau Is.
(N.Z.)

American Samoa
(U.S.A.)

SAMOA

French Polynesia
(Fr.)

TONGA Niue
(N.Z.) Cook Is.
(N.Z.)

Pitcairn Is.
(U.K.)

Tropic of Capricorn

PARAGUAY

Asunción

C
H
I
L
E

A
R
G
E
N
T
I
N
A

URUGUAY

Santiago Buenos
Aires Montevideo

Falkland Is. (U.K.)
•Stanley

South Georgia
(U.K.)

The continents and oceans

North
America

NORTH
ATLANTIC
OCEAN

Europe

Asia

PACIFIC
OCEAN

PACIFIC
OCEAN

Africa

INDIAN
OCEAN

South
America

SOUTH
ATLANTIC
OCEAN

Oceania

SOUTHERN OCEAN

Antarctica

Population of the world's continents

- ◆ Asia   3.64 billion
- ◆ Africa   0.78 billion
- ◆ Europe   0.73 billion
- ◆ N America   0.48 billion
- ◆ S America   0.34 billion
- ◆ Oceania   0.03 billion

The world's top five languages
(native speakers)

- ◆ Chinese (Mandarin)   885 million
- ◆ Hindi   375 million
- ◆ Spanish   358 million
- ◆ English   347 milion
- ◆ Arabic   347 milion

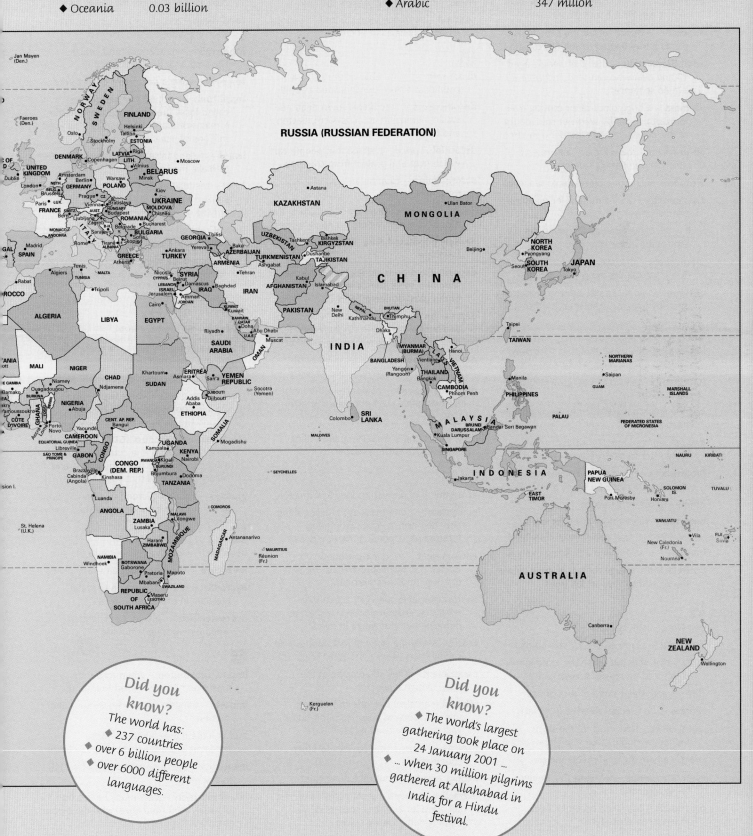

Did you know?
The world has:
- ◆ 237 countries
- ◆ over 6 billion people
- ◆ over 6000 different languages.

Did you know?
- ◆ The world's largest gathering took place on 24 January 2001 ...
- ◆ ... when 30 million pilgrims gathered at Allahabad in India for a Hindu festival.

Glossary

A

abrasion – scraping something away, like sandpaper does

acid rain – rain with acidic gases dissolved in it; it can kill fish and plants

adapted – changed to suit the conditions; plants have adapted to suit the climate

adult literacy rate – the % of people aged 15 and over who can read and write a simple sentence

air mass – a huge block of air moving over the Earth; it can be warm or cold, damp or dry, depending on where it came from

air pressure – the weight of air pressing down on the Earth's surface

altitude – height of a place above sea level

anemometer – an instrument for measuring wind speed

arch – the curved outline left when the sea erodes the inside of a cave away

atmosphere – the layer of gas around the Earth; we call the lower part of it air

attrition – how rocks and stones get worn away by banging against each other

B

backwash – the water that rolls back down a beach after a wave has broken

barometer – an instrument for measuring air pressure

bay – a smooth curve of coast between two headlands

beach – an area made of sand or small stones deposited by waves

biodiversity – the variety of plants and animals in a place

biome – a very large ecosystem

birth rate – the number of births in a country in a year, per thousand people

burglary – breaking into a building to steal

buttress roots – large roots that grow above the ground to support tall trees

C

carnivore – eats animals

cash crop – a crop grown for sale abroad

CCTV – closed circuit television, used in shops and on streets to fight crime

cliff – a very steep slope of rock or soil

climate – the average weather in a place

cloud cover – how much of the sky is hidden by cloud; given in eighths (oktas)

coast – where the land meets the sea

common assault – hitting or threatening to hit someone

consumers – they feed on other living things in an ecosystem

convectional rainfall – rain caused by the sun heating the ground; the ground then heats the air which rises to form clouds

crime – an action that breaks the law

criminal – someone who commits a serious crime, or lives a life of crime

D

death rate – the number of deaths in a country in a year, per thousand people

decomposers – they break down dead and waste material in an ecosystem; bacteria and fungii are examples

defensible space – a space that people can watch over and protect from criminals

deforestation – clearing an area of forest for another use

delta – flat area of deposited material at the mouth of a river, where it enters the sea

densely populated area – lots of people live there

deposit – to drop material; waves deposit sand and small stones in sheltered parts of the coast, forming beaches

depression – a weather system made up of two fronts, a warm front chased by a cold one; it brings wet windy weather

developed country – enjoys good public services and a high standard of living

domestic violence – violence in the home; for example a man punching his wife

drought – a shortage of water

drug trafficking – smuggling and selling illegal drugs such as heroin

E

economic – to do with money and finance

ecosystem – a unit made up of living things and their non-living environment; for example a pond, a forest, a desert

environment – everything around you; the air, soil, rivers and climate are part of our natural environment

environmental crime – an action that breaks an environmental law, such as dumping harmful waste in rivers

erosion – wearing away of rock, stones and soil by rivers, waves, the wind or glaciers

escarpment – a tall steep slope at the edge of high land

ethanol – an alcohol made from plant material (such as sugar cane); it burns well so can be used as fuel

exports – things a country sells to other countries

extinct – has died out (like dinosaurs)

extractive reserves – parts of the rainforest set aside for activities such as rubber tapping and growing spices

F

favela – a slum in a South American city

fetch – the length of water the wind blows over, before it meets the coast

food chain – a chain of names and arrows, showing what species feed on

food web – a network of food chains, showing how they link together

forgery – faking a document or signature

fossil fuels – coal, oil and natural gas; called fossil fuels because they are the remains of plants and animals that lived millions of years ago

fraud – making false claims, usually in order to make money

front – the leading edge of an air mass; a warm front means a warm air mass is arriving

frontal rainfall – rain caused when a warm front meets a cold one

fuel – something we use to provide energy; we usually have to burn a fuel to release its energy (except for nuclear fuel)

G

geology – the study of rocks

global warming – the way temperatures around the world are rising

green – does not harm the environment

greenhouse gases – gases like carbon dioxide and methane that trap heat around the Earth, giving global warming

gross domestic product (GDP) – the total wealth produced in a country in a year; it's the total value of all the goods and services produced that year

groynes – barriers of wood or stone down a beach, to stop sand being washed away

H

headland – land that juts out into the sea

herbivore – an animal that eats only plants

hydraulic action – the action of water pressure in breaking up rock

hydroelectricity – electricity generated when a river spins a turbine

I

import subsitution – when a country makes something it used to import

imports – things a country buys from other countries

Indios – the native 'Indians' whose ancestors were the first settlers in Brazil

inequality – the unequal sharing of wealth in a society

infant mortality – how many babies out of every 1000 born alive, who die before their first birthday

intensive farming – aims to produce as much crop or as many animals as possible, on a given piece of land

isolated settlement – a farm or small hamlet quite far from others

L

landslip – a landslide

laterite – a highly weathered soil that bakes in the sun to form a hard layer

latitude – how far a place is north or south of the equator, measured in degrees

life expectancy – how many years a new baby can expect to live, on average

logging – cutting down trees for timber

longshore drift – how sand and other material is carried parallel to the shore, by the waves

M

mental map – a map that you carry in your mind; it might not be very accurate!

meteorologist – a person who studies weather and climate

mugging – a physical attack on a person in the street in order to steal something

multicultural – has many ethnic groups

N

National Grid – the network of power stations and cables that supply our electricity

natural increase – the birth rate minus the death rate, given as a %

Neighbourhood Watch – a scheme where neighbours keep an eye on each others' homes to help prevent crime

North Atlantic Drift – a warm current in the Atlantic Ocean; it keeps our west coast warmer in winter

nuclear fuel – a substance with unstable atoms that break down, giving out a large amount of energy

O

offender – a person who commits a crime (often used for under 18s)

omnivore – eats both plants and animals; most humans are omnivores

OPEC – the Organization of Petroleum Exporting Countries

organized crime – crime that's planned and carried out by a group of people; usually on a large scale and over a long period

P

pastoralists – people who rear grass-eating animals for a living; they move with them to find pasture (grass to eat)

patent – to register a discovery or invention so that you 'own' it by law; then no-one else can copy it unless they pay you

plain – a large area of flat land

pollution – anything that spoils the environment; for example traffic fumes, factory waste, sewage, litter, noise

population – the number of people in a place

population density – the average number of people per square kilometre

population pyramid – a bar graph showing the population divided into males and females in different age groups

precipitation – water falling from the sky; it could fall as rain, hail, sleet or snow

prevailing wind – the wind that blows most often; in the UK it is a south west wind (it blows *from* the south west)

producers – they make their own food from carbon dioxide and water; plants are producers

public enquiry – an enquiry set up to let people give their point of view (for example about plans for a new road)

PV (photovoltaic) cell – a cell that converts sunlight into electricity

R

relief rainfall – rain caused when air is forced to rise over a hill or mountain

renewable resource – a resource that we can grow or make more of; for example wood

resources – things we need to live and work; for example food and fuel

rural area – an area of countryside, where people live on farms and in villages

S

salt marsh – a low-lying marshy area by the sea, with salty water from the tides

satellite image – a picture taken by a camera carried on a satellite

savanna – an ecosystem that is usually hot but with wet and dry seasons

secure accomodation – a type of prison for young offenders

sentence – the punishment for a crime

shingle – small pebbles

slave trade – buying and selling people to work as slaves

social – about people and society (while *economic* is about money and finance)

solar power – power we get by using sunlight as a fuel, for example in PV cells

solution – the dissolving of minerals from a river bed and banks, by the water

sparsely populated area – very few people live there

species – type of plant or animal

spit – a strip of sand or shingle in the sea

stack – a pillar of rock left standing in the sea when the top of an arch collapses

stump – the remains of a stack which the sea has eroded away

sustainable – can be carried on without doing any harm

swash – the water that rushes up the beach when a wave breaks

T

target hardening – installing things to make it harder for criminals to get at their targets (for example steel shutters)

temperature – how hot or cold something is, measured in degrees Centigrade

terrorism – violent acts (like bombings) carried out for political reasons

thermometer – an instrument for measuring temperature

tides – the rise and fall of the sea level, due mainly to the pull of the moon

traffic offences – offences to do with driving and parking vehicles

transport – the carrying away of eroded material by rivers, waves, the wind or glaciers

treaty – an agreement between countries

tropics – the part of the Earth that lies between the Tropic of Cancer (23.5 °N) and the Tropic of Capricorn (23.5 °S)

U

urban area – a built-up area, such as part of a city; it's the opposite of rural

V

vandalism – wilful damage to property; for example smashing up phone boxes

vegetation – all the trees and other plants growing in a place

victim – a person against whom a crime is committed

visibility – the greatest distance you can see, in km or m; on a foggy day in could be just 1 or 2 metres

W

wave-cut notch – a notch cut in a cliff face by the action of waves

wave-cut platform – the flat rocky area left behind when waves erode a cliff away

weather – the state of the atmosphere around us

weathering – the breaking down of rock; it is caused mainly by the weather

wind – air in motion

wind direction – the direction the wind blows *from*

windfarm – a group of wind turbines set up to generate electricity from the wind

wind speed – how fast the wind blows

wind vane – an instrument for showing the wind direction

Index